The First Family

The First Family

INNOCENCE, AWARENESS, ESTRANGEMENT, AND THE NATURE OF EDEN

Bruce Chilton

NATUS BOOKS
BARRYTOWN, NY

Published by Natus Books, 120 Station Hill Road, Barrytown, NY 12507
natusbooks@stationhill.org

Natus Books is a publishing project of the Institute for Publishing Arts, a not-for-profit, tax-exempt organization [501(c)(3)].

Cover and interior design by Alison Wilkes

Print ISBN: 978-1-58177-228-9
Epub ISBN: 978-1-58177-229-6

Library of Congress Control Number: 2023947348

Manufactured in the United States of America

Contents

PROLOGUE
The Yahwists and Their Eden 1

1. Adam
   First Living Being 9

2. Eve
   The Fruit of Desire 29

3. Abel
   New Promise 47

4. Cain
   The First Murder, the First City 65

5. The Serpent
   Language Unravels Eden 85

6. Yahweh
   Conflicted Creator 105

7. Eden
   The Unbroken Presence 123

EPILOGUE 141

ABOUT BRUCE CHILTON 157

The Yahwists and Their Eden

THE BIBLE EMERGED during a process that lasted a millennium, from the courts of David and Solomon in the tenth century BCE to the end of the first century of the Common Era. Many people contributed to the final result. Generations of scribes produced written texts. Oral reciters—performing memorized traditions in settings that included the Temple, royal courts, local festivals, synagogues, and political councils—played a large part in shaping the written work. The written material was largely spoken, at its point of origin and during recitation: well over 90 percent of people in ancient Israel were illiterate.

Among the contributors to the overall composition of the Bible, none is more important than the group of people, both reciters and scribes, who boldly and directly wrote about God by his name: Yahweh. They understood this name to be his unique and personal designation. It refers to a specific deity, the protector of their people. These reciters and writers are known collectively as "the Yahwist" by scholars, better conceived in the plural as the Yahwists, to acknowledge their communal work.

As the biblical period unfolded, designating God by this personal name became taboo, to prevent the name from being used for "vain"—trivial or selfish—purposes (Exodus 20:7). This convention continues in Orthodox and other forms of Judaism to this day. English translations of the Bible have generally followed Rabbinic practice by replacing the name "Yahweh" with another term, most frequently "Lord." That practice poses a problem in understanding the work of the Yahwists. Their Yahweh was a person, not an abstraction, and they felt no embarrassment in their anthropomorphic rendering of his motives. To understand them we need to reflect their usage, and also to convey as directly as possible the vigor of their language. All translations in this volume are fresh, in order to accurately present how the Yahwists conceived of our origins.

Genesis chapters 2 through 4 begin the Yahwists' work. They present a story that is active in our collective memory. It is the story of Eden and the creation of Adam and Eve, their eating of the forbidden fruit, their expulsion from the

Garden, the murder of Abel by Cain, and Cain's banishment, when he is marked by Yahweh and forced to wander the earth.

The original Hebrew text is my focus, although as this book unfolds I also deal with some of the extraordinary interpretations and embellishments the Yahwists have spawned. Part of my work as a scholar has been in ancient languages, and I have seen this story cycle through versions in Aramaic, Greek, Coptic, Latin, and Arabic. It goes without saying that it has had a profound effect on Western culture, catalyzing the imaginations of artists such as Blake, Dante, Michelangelo, and Milton, and shaping the West's religious attitudes and behavior. In my fifty years of pastoral work as an Anglican priest, I have also witnessed how people have personally wrestled with what happens to the first family in the Garden, even as I have grappled with that myself. I have come to see that the Yahwists' work needs to be understood in its own terms, if we are to understand how the story has been reshaped over time, and incorporated within our individual psychologies and collective imagination. That is what I have tried to do here.

The Yahwists never bothered to identify themselves. Attempts have been made by various scholars to invent a biography of the author as a man or woman in the court of David or of Solomon. The Yahwists' work has also been attributed to the court of Solomon's son Rehoboam. These speculations are interesting. But it is far more straightforward and consistent with the evidence, as developed in the most recent scholarship of how the Bible was formed,[1] to see the Yahwists' epic as the collective work of several generations who crafted a vision of a particular relationship between their people and God.

The Yahwists told the story of the creation of Eden and the drama that happened there as the first instalment of an epic. Their saga encompassed other episodes in Israel's history: Noah's Flood, the Tower of Babel, how Abraham was called by Yahweh and entered into a covenant with him and with his sons Isaac and Jacob. Yahweh brought Israel out of Egypt, sent local leaders called judges to preserve Israel's heritage and land, and personally chose David and his dynasty to govern his people.

The epic begins as the Yahwists introduce us to Adam, Eve, Abel, Cain, the Serpent, and Yahweh. Later interpretations of the biblical text would make each of the characters into something new. Adam would become the first sinner and Eve the first seductress; Abel became a template of Christ and Cain his primordial betrayer; the Serpent acquired metaphysical status as Satan; and

---

[1] At the end of this Prologue, and of each chapter of the book, short notes provide a bibliography for those who wish to trace critical discussion further.

Yahweh exchanged an anthropomorphic personality for the claim that he was omniscient and omnipotent. Eden itself became the faint memory of a previous world rather than the tangible place that the Yahwists describe. And yet Eden lingers in our memory as a place of innocence, abundance, and ease, and, perhaps, a place to which it might be possible to return. Each time we refer to Eden we reconnect with its promise. We will briefly discuss these issues in the Epilogue so as not to distract too much from the Yahwists' native conceptions and the original story itself, which are our primary areas of interest.

The Yahwists' contribution to the Hebrew Bible is often called the "Yahwist Source" or "J Source," with the "J" deriving from the German transcription of the first letter of the name Yahweh (since German scholarship in the nineteenth century originally identified this source). I am not fully convinced that the Yahwists' traditions were all written before incorporation into the Bible. My personal estimate is that the Yahwists were provoked to begin their work under the stress of the revolt of Jeroboam, when the northern part of the kingdom that David had founded seceded from Judea in the south and formed a separate nation by the end of the tenth century BCE. That painful schism threatened the Davidic monarchy without destroying it. The punishment of Adam, who was banished from the Garden and yet could continue to live from the skills he learned there on much less promising ground, seems to me to be at least in part a mirror of the painful loss by David's dynasty of some of its most prosperous lands.

Focus on the Yahwists as creators of the saga of first family raises the question of the majestic first chapter of Genesis, which opens, unforgettably, with the words "In the beginning God created the heavens and the earth" and articulates a cosmological drama that unfolds when the spirit of God moves upon the face of the deep. This more sophisticated creation story was produced by a different author or authors who came four centuries later than the Yahwists and whom scholars identify as "P," or the Priestly Source, which concerns itself with issues of sacrifice, holiness, and purity. A consensus of scholarship sees the Priestly project as putting together not only the Book of Genesis in the sixth century BCE but the first five books of the Torah, the Pentateuch.

Genesis chapter 1 functions as a kind of prologue to the saga of the first family. The Priestly stream had its own interpretation of what happened in the beginning, but its compilers let the Yahwist story stand. The resulting enjambment—its contradictions and the mystery of beginning the story of the beginning only to begin it again in Genesis chapter 2—has pollinated millennia of interpretation, including this account.

The story of Eden is one of innocence, suffering,

estrangement, displacement, self-consciousness, awakening, separation. But it is also a story of hope, about gaining wisdom and self-knowledge. It is about the price of acquiring knowledge, about the costs of maturation and a reckoning with our own mortality. The Yahwist story ultimately, inevitably takes us out of Eden into a world of toil and bloodshed and death. But my purpose in this book has been to present the other part of their Edenic vision, which is also present. This is a vision of a near, knowable Eden, which was palpable for the Yahwists and lingers to this day. It promises a world of genuine humanity that endures in our hearts and imaginations, whatever the world of experience might suggest.

This book was inspired by Laszlo Z. Bito's *Eden Revisited: A Novel*, published by the Institute of Advanced Theology at Bard College, which I founded and direct, and Natus Books. Laszlo's richly imagined alternative story of Eden deliberately departs from the biblical plot, and yet at the same time targets the nexus of relationships that is also the Yahwists' center of attention. Laszlo invites us to see that the primordial power of the story resides in forces that still move around us and within us. Both Laszlo's book and mine have seen the light of day owing to crucial support: Olivia Bito's conceptual clarity, Kenneth Wapner's editorial acumen, Sam Truit's expertise in production, and Melissa Germano's logistical prowess. As has been the case before, the Institute of Advanced Theology gave me a hearing in oral presentations that permitted the project to emerge.

The First Family is a story of resilience and endurance, of being frustrated and thwarted and adjusting, finding a new way. It is about becoming conscious, with an awareness of the light and dark, the good and bad. The saga of the first family shows us that the promise of Eden may have been damaged, but it has not lost.

NOTE:

For an accessible, clear, and scholarly reconstruction of the Yahwists' work in regard to the Pentateuch, see Richard Elliott Friedman, *The Bible with Sources Revealed. A New View into the Five Books of Moses* (New York: HarperSanFrancisco, 2003). Facing up to the fashion against speaking of the Yahwists at all, *The Book of J* by David Rosenberg and Harold Bloom (New York: Grove Weidenfeld, 1990) is a fine and attractive contribution. A more academic and detailed analysis is offered in Joel S. Baden, "Continuity: The J Source," *The Composition of the Pentateuch. Renewing the Documentary Hypothesis* (New Haven: Yale University Press, 2012) 45–81.

1.

Adam
First Living Being

> "Yahweh formed the 'Adam, dust from the 'Adamah, and breathed the breath of life in his nostrils, and the 'Adam became a living being." GENESIS 2.7

THE YAHWISTS OPEN their epic of how Israel began by relating how people as a whole came to be. As explained in the Prologue, the first chapter of Genesis comes from the later, Priestly source, the brilliant group of redactors who put together the text as we know it during the Babylonian captivity in the sixth century BCE. Instead of starting with the earth being formless (Genesis 1:2), the Yahwists describe the earth as not yet having any growth (Genesis 2:4-5). That is because the interest of the Yahwists is not in producing a complete cosmology but in showing how what they call the "bringings forth" or "generations" of life

9

began to unfold through history (Genesis 2:4); it is a story of human interactions and relationships which takes for granted the physical existence of the earth. The Yahwists' cosmology was practical rather than speculative, and yet it is also daring.

According to the Yahwists the generative point of life was not a plant or an animal, but 'Adam, a term that means "man." In calling the first man 'adam, the article "the" (a simple ha-sound in Hebrew) appears before 'adam in Genesis. Used in that way, "the Adam" is both a generic designation and the identity of a specific character. The Yahwists press the meaning of 'adam further: man is shaped from dust from the "earth," 'adamah. 'Adamah can be used in the sense of the substance of the world, its dry land, and also as "soil." Much of the uncultivated earth in the Near East is red-tinged with a high content of clay, and the word 'edôm, "red," is related to 'Adamah. Red in the soil and red in the veins are causally associated for the Yahwists; in their minds, life comes from the earth. That symbiosis echoes for the Yahwists each time the term "Adam" appears.

The link is so deep between 'Adamah and 'Adam that one cannot flourish without the other. In the Yahwists' cosmology, the earth ('Adamah) needs man ('Adam), because otherwise –difficult though this is to imagine– there would be no plant life. This view is plainly stated, but it is so contrary to how the emergence of life is understood today that it takes a moment to appreciate what the Yahwists are saying. By carefully following the text, we can understand its meaning:

> No plant of the field was yet on the *'Adamah*, and no grass of the field had sprouted, because Yahweh had not made it rain on the *'Adamah* and there was no *'Adam* to work the *'Adamah*. (Genesis 2:5)

Adam's origin and purpose are bound to the earth. He is as necessary as rain, according to the description of the Yahwists, in the emergence of plants. Adam's powerful agency in making the earth green has been frequently overlooked by interpreters, who have focused on the totally different order of Genesis 1, where plant life precedes all animal life and people appear only at the end of the process. Genesis chapter 1 skews their reading of Genesis 2. So it is that much of the story of the first family, who they are and their legacy, has been obscured.

The Yahwists assert that working the earth is necessary for fertility. Growth happens because of people. Yahweh cures the earth of its barrenness by watering the ground and making Adam. Human beings will live from what grows. Plants become possible only because the man works the soil. The creation of animal life comes later in the story.

In the equally pre-scientific view of Genesis 1, plant life precedes not only animal life but also the creation of the sun and the moon; animal life comes before human life, and people are made male and female from the outset (Genesis 1:11–27).

Enormous effort has been expended to make these two different accounts of creation, in Genesis chapters 1 and 2, say the same thing. But they have failed. In the Yahwists' account, humans frame the whole process of the creation of the world, at its beginning and its end, and Yahweh intervenes personally and physically at every stage of the process. This is not at all what happens in Genesis 1.

Once Adam is created, Yahweh can make a luxuriant garden in a place called *'Eden*. The name, in its most basic sense, means "pleasure"; here Yahweh puts the man he has formed (Genesis 2:8, 15). The whole of the land of Eden cradles life. The Yahwists describe a mammoth river that flows from Eden and waters the Garden. It then divides into the four great rivers of the world: the Tigris and Euphrates in Mesopotamia, the Pishon (or Nile) in Egypt, and the Gihon (or the Wādī al-Ḥamḍ) in Saudi Arabia. Eden, in other words, is the source of all life, a nourishing source that connects the known civilizations of the time through their rivers, even though these rivers were not visibly connected (Genesis 2:10–14).

The Yahwists speak of the Garden and its primordial

river as lying somewhere to the east within Eden (Genesis 2:8). This one of several steps east that the story will describe, as Adam and Eve will be expelled to the east of Eden itself (Genesis 3:24) and then Cain leaves the presence of Yahweh to live farther eastward still (Genesis 4:16). From this perspective, the Israelites in the fledgling kingdom of David and Solomon, centered in Jerusalem, had come from the east, and in their view that is where humanity originated, in the ancient land generally known now as Sumer.

Eden will be closed to people, but its vitality was so great that all known civilizations lived from its waters. The Yahwists conception is that Eden's overflow continued to provide life. When he was still in Eden, Adam's life was idyllic and rewarding, bound up with the promise of his intimate connection with Yahweh, who had provided the Garden with "every tree pleasant for sight and good for food, even the Tree of Life in the Garden's midst and the Tree of the Knowledge of Good and Evil" (Genesis 2:9).

The last of all these trees, of course, will produce dire consequences for humanity. But before describing what happened when people absorbed more knowledge than they were designed for, the Yahwists stress God's command that "you shall indeed eat from every tree of the Garden" (Genesis 2:16). The plenty is immeasurable and the sense of pleasure limitless.

We might ask: why are two trees—Life and Knowledge—singled out? The Yahwists followed the great mythologies of the ancient world that celebrated the majesty of trees and often associated them with both enduring life and wisdom. The imagery reflects the understanding: both Life and Knowledge are literally planted by Yahweh in the world.

The Tree of the Knowledge of Good and Evil will, of course, upset Yahweh's arrangements in the Garden, and that poses the question of why he planted it there in the first place. In a standard understanding of the classical Hebrew of Genesis, the reference to knowing "Good" (*tôv*) and "Evil" (*ra'*) refers to a spectrum of understanding, running the gamut from good at one end to evil or bad at the other. The phrase conveys the range of our experience. Similar wording, including the term *ra'* for bad or evil, appears in the Book of Isaiah. Yahweh says that he himself is:

> "The one who forms light and creates dark,
> makes peace and creates conflict (*ra'*)." (Isaiah 45:7)

As in the case of the Tree of Knowledge, the meaning of the term *ra'* depends on what lies at the other end of the comparison. In Isaiah, *ra'* is the antonym of *shalom*. So if *shalom* is rendered "peace," *ra'* should be conflict, or some other warlike state. But *shalom* itself carries a broad swath of meaning, so that *ra'* here has also been rendered, in published translations, as "disaster," "calamity," "doom," "woe," "sorrow," and "trouble," as well as "evil."

Translators of the Bible need to adjust to the reality that there is no one-to-one correspondence between the language we speak and any other language. In the case of ancient languages, this is all the more the case, when the views of the world and of what makes a human truly human are radically different from our own. Even when an ancient language has later derivatives, such as the Romance languages (from Latin), Coptic (from Egyptian), modern Hebrew (from Classical Hebrew), and modern Greek (from the Attic and Koinê versions of Antiquity), that does not mean that what came later can determine what was said many centuries ago. Language is malleable, subject to sometimes rapid changes of usage and sense. The term *ra'*, in particular, was flexibly used in the Hebrew Bible.

This flexibility has also resulted in great differences in rendering the phrase about the Tree of Knowledge in Genesis 2:9 to include: "Good and Evil," "Right and Wrong," "Blessing and Calamity," "Good and Bad," and variations on those choices. None of these renderings are false, but justice will be done to the Hebrew original only if the idea of a spectrum or range of knowledge is kept in mind. In English, the rendering "evil" sometimes produces a misunderstanding. Because that term carries with it a moral sense which is stronger in its negative connotation than the term "good" is in its positive connotations, English speakers can draw the conclusion that the Tree of Knowledge represents wickedness.

That is not what the phrasing signifies in Classical Hebrew. The Book of Isaiah, for example, imagines that every child comes to a point in development that involves making choices about what to eat. Speaking of a child who is yet to be born, the prophet predicts judgment that will come upon the community when that child has reached this stage of development:

> He shall eat butter and honey when he knows
> to reject bad things and choose good things.
> (Isaiah 7:15)

Again, the wording of translations varies, but there is agreement that the sense is of a child who has reached the moment of making conscious decisions. That, as we will see, is also involved in eating the fruit of the Tree of Knowledge.

One of the greatest philosophers of Judaism, Maimonides (1138-1204), explains the significance of Adam's eating from the Tree in his *Guide to the Perplexed*. He points out that, from the moment of his creation,

Adam's rational intelligence is perfect. He knows how to work the Garden; he can understand when Yahweh speaks to him; he gives names to all the animals that God creates, and to the first Woman, as well (Genesis 2:15-23). Maimonides reasons that the Tree of Knowledge does not refer to rational intelligence at all. Instead of dealing with the true and false, the purview of rationality, the Tree stands for preferences and appetites, things that are liked, which are deemed "good," and things that are disliked, or "bad." Adam actually loses intelligence when he eats the fruit of the Tree because he replaces his rational intelligence with a conventional preference for likes and dislikes: the "Knowledge" referred to in the text is not generic, but indicates a *way* of knowing.

There is an inevitability to how things unfold when people and gods are at cross purposes. In Genesis, Yahweh sets out one and only one fateful condition for Eden's idyll of human existence to continue. Yahweh tells Adam, "from the Tree of the Knowledge of Good and Evil, from that you shall not eat, because in the day you eat from that you shall indeed die" (Genesis 2:17).

The "Knowledge" that the Man and the Woman gain has to do with a deepening of their awareness of themselves. At that moment, "their eyes were opened, and they knew that they were naked" (Genesis 3:7). The new way of knowing that Maimonides alerts us to is not quite, as he thought, appetites and desires, but shameful self-conscious-ness. That awareness is a burden all its own, but it is not at all commensurate with the threat of immediate death. They do not die; rather, Yahweh takes another tack:

> Yahweh said, "Look—Adam has become like one
> of us, knowing good and evil. Now, so he does not
> stretch his hand out and take also from the Tree of
> Life and eat and live forever . . ." (Genesis 3:22)

Without finishing that sentence, Yahweh sends Adam on his way. Yahweh does not want Adam to become even more like him, by living forever as well as knowing good and evil. His thought process shows that two Trees, one of Life and the other of Knowledge, are at issue, so that interpretations that conceive of a single plant under two names are not supported. Yahweh's speaks as if he had an audience among other divine figures. "Look—Adam has become like one of us," he says. That "us" refers to a divine class of beings.

At this early stage in the development of the religion of Israel, monotheism had not yet emerged. The belief that there is one and only one God anywhere, a daring assertion that denies the ambient polytheism of Antiquity, came to voice in the Book of Isaiah in the sixth century BCE: "I am Yahweh, and there is no other, apart from me there is no god" (Isaiah 45:5). Before the time of that audacious but profoundly influential announcement, the Israelite tradition was not monotheist but henotheist: that is, Israel was held to loyalty to Yahweh alone, without the claim no other god existed. For this reason, that "us" in Genesis 3:22 evoked a pantheistic divinity, which is distinct from humanity. Yahweh refers to a boundary he does not want breached. After the period of the Yahwists, usages of the plural were strictly understood as what is called a plural of majesty, but that equivalent of the royal "we" awaited the emergence of monotheism to become firmly established.

Yahweh is, quite simply, jealous of his own status. That trait is fully endorsed by the Yahwists, because, as they remind their hearers, "You shall not worship another god, because Yahweh, his name is jealous: he is a jealous God" (Exodus 34:14). His jealousy both excluded the worship of other gods and insisted upon Yahweh's status as divine rather than human. However anthropomorphic he might be, he had not been created from the earth, but was the author of the first being.

Adam has eaten from the tree, and Yahweh is about to mete out punishment. But before that happens, we need to retrace our steps, circling backward and filling in a crucial aspect of the story we have skipped over—crucially, the creation of Eve, and Eve's interaction with the Serpent, to which Adam is a strangely passive observer.

In the sequence of creation, after Adam names the animals but before he eats the fruit, Yahweh realizes that "it is not good for the Adam to be alone" (Genesis 2:18). Yahweh decides to make a partner for him. Only at this point does Yahweh set about creating animals. He makes beasts of the field and birds of the air from the ground, exactly as he had formed Adam. Yahweh makes the creatures and brings them to Adam to see what he would call them, and Adam names them (Genesis 2:19-20).

The experiment of producing animals and birds as candidates to be Adam's partner fails: Adam does not find "a counterpart partner" (*'ēzer negedô*; Genesis 2:20). That phrase is a compound, combining the noun *'ēzer*, "support" or "partner" with the phrase "corresponding to him," *negedô*. The latter phrase is built upon the preposition *neged*, which refers to what stands before one as an equal. Yahweh has produced animals—such as oxen and asses—that could help Adam with his work. But they were not true counterparts.

That changes with Yahweh's creation of the first Woman. Now, for the first time, Yahweh makes one creature from another. He fashions a partner, not from the ground, as in the case of every other act of creation, but sends Adam into a deep sleep and creates new life from Adam's own bone and flesh (Genesis 2:21-22). Adam names the result:

> This time it is bone of my bone and flesh
> of my flesh;
> she will be called Woman, because she is taken
> from Man. (Genesis 2:23)

Obviously, there are subordinating implications for "Woman" in this depiction, and we will take them up further along. For the moment, however, our focus will be on the Yahwists' emphasis. The production of woman from man determines how society is organized: "a man shall leave his father and his mother and adhere to his woman, and they shall be one flesh. (Genesis 2:24)

This explanation is for a future time, of course. There are not yet mothers and fathers or choices about where to live. The chapter concludes, "They were both naked, the 'Adam and his woman, and they had no shame" (Genesis 2:25). This implies that the idyllic quality in the garden extended into the first couple's sexual relations. Commenting on this verse, the Jewish sage Rashi (1040–1105) remarked that before the people ate the fruit and became self-conscious, their sexuality was spontaneous. After the couple eats from the Tree of Knowledge, however, "the eyes of the two of them were opened, and they knew that they were naked and they stitched fig leaves together and made themselves loin-covers" (Genesis 3:7). Yahweh, once the fruit has been consumed, does not respond immediately. He is walking about in the Garden to enjoy the cool evening breeze. Yahweh is not omniscient: "Where are you?" he asks Adam (Genesis 3:8–9). Adam explains that he had hidden himself; he was afraid because he knew he was naked. Yahweh asks, "Who told you that you were naked? Did you eat from the tree I commanded you not to eat from?" (Genesis 3:10–11).

The shame Adam feels might have been considered adequate punishment in itself. But then Adam compounds his fault by saying:

> "The Woman you gave me, alongside me, she gave me from the tree, and I ate." (Genesis 3:12)

The woman follows suit by blaming the Serpent (Genesis 3:13). Yahweh cuts into any further explanations by cursing the three characters.

In this scene, the Yahwists address one of the central themes in their epic as a whole: the qualities that Yahweh values and those that irritate him. Yahweh's fierce response to Adam's attempt to shirk responsibility might seem extreme. After all, the experience of shame brings with it an awareness of one's guilt, and therefore the reflex of covering it up.

But the idea of shame for the Yahwists had a larger dimension that transcended the psychological or emotional. The word for "shame," *bôsht* in Hebrew, had deep resonance. It refers in a simple sense to the feeling of being ashamed; the statement in Genesis 2:25 that Adam and the Woman were naked and yet had no shame, for example, takes a verbal form of the same term (*lô' yit-bôshshu*). But Israelites also associated the god Baal—who competed with Yahweh—with the term "shame." Priests of Baal, unlike priests of Yahweh, were known to engage in sacrifice naked, and sacred prostitution featured in Baalism. In response, Israelites often replaced the name Baal with *bôsht*, the sort of play with the names of opponents that frequently arises during prolonged conflicts. This replacement language was allied also to a competitor to the Yahwists' hero, King David. In order to come to power, he needed to get past the son of his predecessor, King Saul. Saul's son was named "Eshbaal" (1 Chronicles 8:33), which means "fire of Baal." Instead, the Yahwists called him "Ishbosht," or "man of shame" (2 Samuel 2:10).

Yahweh and David were inextricably related in the minds of the Yahwists, such that to deny one was to deny the other. They composed their work at a time and place when Israel's success was due to David. David was their hero at every stage in their work. Yet David was flawed. He committed adultery with Bathsheba while her husband, Uriah, did battle on David's behalf, and then arranged to have Uriah killed (2 Samuel chapters 11–12). When the prophet Nathan rebukes David for his behavior, David repents, and Nathan conveys Yahweh's mercy:

> David said to Nathan, "I have sinned against Yahweh." Nathan said to David, "Now Yahweh has put away your sin: you shall not die."
> (2 Samuel 12:13)

David does exactly what Adam did not do—acknowledge his own guilt.

In Eden and for the Yahwists, the worst failure is not disobedience, but not taking responsibility for disobedience. It is when Adam shirks blame after eating the fruit that Yahweh reacts in anger:

> "Because you have listened to the voice of your Woman,
> and ate from the tree that I commanded you,
> saying, 'You shall not eat from it,'
> Cursed is the ground because of you:
> By labor shall you eat all the days of your life:
> It will sprout thorn and thistle for you,
> And you will eat the grass of the field.
> By the sweat of your brow you shall eat bread until you return to the ground:

Since you were taken from it, so you are dust, and
to dust you shall return." (Genesis 3:17-19)

Those opening words, "Because you have listened to the
voice of your Woman," obviously carry with them the
assumption that males should be in a position of authority
in relation to females, an aspect of the Yahwists' perspective
that will be further emphasized by what Yahweh does to
the woman. In addition, Yahweh calls attention to Adam's
strange passivity.

Yet Adam is not directly cursed; instead, the ground is.
Where once luxuriant fruit trees sprouted, now there will
be thorn and thistle. Food will now come by cultivating
"grass of the field"—grain, in other words, and milling that
grain for bread. Bread, long the staple diet of Israelites by
the time of the Yahwist, requires cultivation, hard work,
time, and fire to produce.

The burden of living by the sweat of one's brow does
not end until life ends. It is made clear here for the first
time that Adam is mortal: he will return to the same earth
from which he was created. To assure that, Yahweh expels
Adam from the Garden, to prevent him from having access
to the Tree of Life (Genesis 3:22-24). A flaming sword and
mythic beasts called Cherubim, as fearsome as the griffins
of medieval heraldry, block Adam's way to that tree. They
block our way back as well—apparently forever.

The Yahwists explain Adam's catastrophic loss of Paradise in terms of passive inadvertence rather than deliberate rebellion. By not engaging with the Serpent and the Woman, Adam conceals himself in silence before he does so physically. When he does speak, as we have seen, it is to try to wheedle away from owning his action by blaming "the Woman" (Genesis 3:12). His thought process is not in any way indicated at the moment of eating the fruit: at that crucial juncture, he is not an agent of action but its passive recipient. A certain indulgence, coupled with a tendency to go along with ill-considered advice, led to Adam's painful failure. He survived his failure and continued to be an actor in events, although in a reduced role.

Adam speaks once more in Genesis, after the curse of the ground is pronounced but before the expulsion from the Garden. He names the woman *Ḥavah* in Hebrew, which comes into English as "Eve." He also gives the reason for the name: "because she was the mother of all living (*Ḥay*)" (Genesis 3:20).

Once out of the Garden, Adam is referred to in Genesis (4:1, 25; 5:5) only in connection to fathering children and his death at the age of 930 years. His passivity becomes a principal trait of his character, standing in contrast to his engaged involvement with Yahweh's creation of all the animals from the earth and with Yahweh's surprising decision to fashion Adam's partner from Adam's own body. He became the archetype of those who worked the fields at the time of the Yahwists: physically spent, laboring for results that the earth seemed determined to deny them, and yet aware that the scarcity of the ground they tilled hinted at the limitless fertility of a land from which they had been banished.

From prehistory into the present of Yahwists, agriculture required tilling, watering, pruning, weeding, and nurturing. Crops periodically failed—hunger and even starvation were always possibilities. The ethos of Adam was that of the Yahwists. They looked back in their epic to a time and place when Eden was here and now—an abundant paradise. God walked in the cool of the evening and human beings easily and effortlessly reaped the Garden's fruits. How different from the hard labor of producing grain out of a hard land. The Yahwists' epic portrays Israel's difficult life on the edge of survival as the vestige of an idyllic past. Safeguarding the residue of a once effortless creation meant maintaining a good relationship with Yahweh. Part of that was remembering why Yahweh had expelled Adam from the Garden, and how Israel was still living in the shadow of exile.

NOTE:

For Adam's role as an archetype, and the millennial attempt to reconcile Genesis 1 and Genesis 2 in their accounts of creation, see Peter Schäfer, "Adam," *The Jewish Jesus: How Judaism and Christianity Shaped Each Other* (Princeton: Princeton University Press, 2012), 197–213. The rise of Fundamentalism in the United States has resulted in attempts to portray Adam as a historical figure, while the Yahwists clearly present him as an archetype. The anachronisms involved in identifications of Adam with, for example, *Homo heidelbergensis*, have been well explained by Paul Korchin in his review of William Lane Craig, *In Quest of the Historical Adam: A Biblical and Scientific Exploration* (Grand Rapids: Eerdmans, 2021), which is available in *The Review of Biblical Literature* (https://www.sblcentral.org/home/rbl; March 2023).

2.

Eve
The Fruit of Desire

The Woman saw that the tree was good for food and that it was a delight to the eyes and desirable to enlighten; she took from its fruit and ate and gave to her man, and he ate. GENESIS 3:6

WE HAVE LEFT Adam banished to the labor involved in what Laszlo Bito called the Outerworld, a term I take up here. The way back to Eden is guarded by Cherubim with a flaming sword. Adam is not alone, of course. By his side stands Eve. They face their new life and their fate together. Both have been designated with the roles they will play in the future of humanity: Adam as a tiller of soil, the provider; Eve, as we shall see, as the giver of human life.

This is the account in the saga of the first couple that the Yahwists have given to us in Genesis chapters 2–4.

We will consider some of the ins and outs of that account in due course, but before we do, I want to consider what comes before it—the vision of male-female relations presented in the Priestly source of Genesis chapter 1.

The subservient Eve of the Yahwists conflicts with the coequal female role given to women by the Priestly source. The Priestly source is clear: both man and women are created in the image of God; together they will enjoy the fruits of the earth and their mastery of over other creatures, and they will be blessed with children. This is the vision of Genesis' first chapter:

> God created the *'Adam* in his own image, in the
> image of God he created him: masculine and
> feminine he created them. And God blessed them,
> and God said to them, "Be fertile and multiply
> and fill the earth and tame it, and subdue the
> fish of the sea and the birds of the heavens and
> every living thing that moves upon the ground."
> (Genesis 1:27–28)

Male and the female are *both* explicitly and simultaneously commanded. The Hebrew terms involved are telling: the word "masculine" (*zakar*) and "feminine" (*neqêbah*) are not related in the way "man" and "woman" are, which is how the Yahwist initially refers to the first couple. The

English terms male and female, usually used in published translations, are also deceptive; "masculine" and "feminine" capture the sense better as terms that are coequal.

Although the Hebrew Bible is often portrayed as a uniformly patriarchal and misogynistic text, there is another strand that runs through it, although not as often recognized. Picking up the Priestly vision of Genesis chapter 1, a latter strand of the Hebrew Bible portrays Wisdom as feminine, an aspect of divinity that is a primordial Spirit that infuses creation and shapes it.

Before the existence of Israel, many civilizations had prized Wisdom as a quality that linked the divine world and the human world. This ancient conception was embraced within the Hebrew Bible only as a result of a major development of thought that occurred well after the period of the Yahwists, during the sixth century BCE. "Wisdom" in the Hebrew language is *Hôkmah,* which is a feminine noun. That opened the way to personifying Wisdom as the feminine aspect of God. As we see in the quote above from the first chapter of Genesis, God created humanity in God's own image, and that creation involves both masculine and feminine human beings. This implies that God also included both male and female.

Following this chain of thought was virtually impossible, at least openly, during the long period when Yahweh was understood among Israelites to be in conflict with other gods. While some of them, such as Dagon, were male gods, others, such as Astarte, were goddesses. Worship of Astarte is specifically condemned (see Judges 2:13–14; 10:6–7; 1 Samuel 7:34; 12:10; 31:10; 1 Kings 11:5, 33; 2 Kings 23:13; Jeremiah 7:18; 44:17–19, 25), but that condemnation is so forceful, repetitive, and specific that it has long been evident that some Israelites were attracted to Astarte herself and goddesses like her, which had been part of the Canaanite pantheon before Israel was established. Indeed, Israelite attraction to feminine goddesses was a likely part of the motivation of the Yahwist in demoting the status of Eve and making her subservient to Adam.

As long as Yahweh was seen in competition with goddesses, the idea of associating the feminine with the divine was rejected as a form of disloyalty to the God of Israel. Although the existence of other gods was taken for granted, he alone was held to be Israel's protector and deity. But during the sixth century BCE, Israelite theology, shaped by the prophets and priests and scribes and poets who first put the Hebrew Bible into a form we would recognize today, went through a radical change. The conviction grew that Yahweh was not only the God for Israel but in fact the only God. The Book of Isaiah marks this epochal moment, by having God say:

"I am Yahweh, there is not another: besides me
there is no God." (Isaiah 45:5)

Monotheism was born and exerted a profound influence
on the religions of the world. But as a consequence, because
the sense of competition was removed, ancient ideas that
has long been repressed could be explored, and in some
cases valued. Wisdom emerged as Yahweh's consort, not as
his nemesis.

The Book of Proverbs brings together traditions collected over centuries that were designed to teach Israelites,
from the humble to the most aristocratic, how to live. Some
of the material in Proverbs represents the new daring
of monotheism in discovering the feminine face of the
divine. In its eighth chapter, Proverbs brilliantly associates
Wisdom with God's Spirit, since the latter is also a feminine
term (*ruah*). Here Wisdom herself speaks, establishing
her identity:

Yahweh created me, the beginning of his course,
first of his works of old. I was set up primordially,
at first, before the earth's foundations. When there
were no depths, I was brought forth, when there
were no springs gushing waters. Before the moun-
tains were shaped, before the hills, I was brought
forth; before he made the earth and open space

and the first dust of the world. When he established the heavens I was there, when he inscribed
a circle on the face of the deep, when he located
the clouds above and secured the fountains of
the deep, when he set the limit of the sea, so
waters shall not transgress his command, when he
decreed the foundations of the earth–I was with
him, an architect, and I was delight, day after day,
rejoicing before him always, rejoicing in the world
of his earth, and my delight was with the sons of
men. (Proverbs 8:22–31)

At the beginning of Genesis, God's Spirit moves over the
face of the primeval waters (Genesis 1:2). Proverbs provides
an explanation for how the Spirit, as Wisdom, took part in
this initial episode of creation. As God conceives what creation is to be, his intent is Wisdom–the conception he will
follow. She is the first of his creations, the primordial center
of all that is. Because she personifies the divine intention
in creating, she takes on the role of an "architect" ('amôn in
Hebrew). The term carries associations with Egyptian and
resonates with a wider Near Eastern conception of a feminine presence woven into creation.

In sharp contrast to the later conceptions involving
Wisdom, the Yahwists present Yahweh as acting entirely on
his own. Once Adam has been ensconced in the Garden,

Yahweh is concerned that Adam is alone, and that this condition is not good for him (Genesis 2:18). That makes Yahweh create the whole range of animals, searching for a suitable partner for Adam.

Adam and every creature in the Garden have been produced directly from the dust of the Earth. That is not the case with Eve. Eve is actually made out of *flesh*. And Adam himself, who as we've already noted is in a position to know, emphasizes this by what he says. Unlike all those other times when he saw the various creatures that were brought before him, "this time it is bone of my bone and flesh of my flesh. For this reason she shall be called Woman, because she was taken from Man." Adam says that he is a "man" (an *'ish*) so that he calls what has been made from his flesh and bone a "woman" (*'ishah*), since she was taken from a man (Genesis 2:23). That language, of course, explicitly makes the woman an auxiliary figure. Adam's partner is designated by the Hebrew term *'êzer,* which might also be translated as "support"; the King James Version renders the Hebrew word "help meet." Both translations reveal what is already in the original wording, a gendered hierarchy. Adam is made to serve the earth, and his partner is created to provide him with support.

Yahweh, in order to make Eve, puts Adam into a heavy sleep, so as to remove both bone and flesh from his side (Genesis 2:22-23). In the conception of the Yahwists, people most closely encounter Yahweh when they are in deep torpor: the exact term for "heavy sleep" (*tardemah*) is also used when Abraham is made the beneficiary of a unique covenant with Yahweh (Genesis 15:12–21). The term for "side" can also mean "rib," and is often translated in that way. But Rashi rightly points out that more than literal bone is at issue in this special act of creation, so that it must mean "side," a usage that is well established in Hebrew.

Embedded within this latent and explicit subservience in the partner's identity is nonetheless an emphatically unique aspect of the Woman's creation. Adam and every other creature have been produced directly from the dust of the Earth (Genesis 2:7, 19). That is not the case with Woman. Woman is made from flesh from the very outset. She is not, by her identity in creation, dedicated to tilling the earth in the same way that Adam is. Even if her role is subservient, her being belongs to the world of human society, not to agriculture. That is why the Yahwists go on to say, "Therefore, a man leaves his father and mother and joins his woman and they become one flesh" (Genesis 2:24).

The implications of a man changing households were woven deep within the structure of the ancient Middle Eastern world of the Yahwist. Iron Age Israel, with its subsistence agricultural economy, depended on the kind of work that Adam had been made for, and that had become much more difficult after he disobeyed Yahweh and then attempted to evade responsibility for his disobedience. Family relationships were literally grounded in the soil, and a man's departing the household of his parents meant that his labor was lost to his birth family. Marriage is here presented as being a relationship that breaks the ordinary tie that there is between a man and the ground of his birth family. This model applies to most of the history of Israel until well after the first century, when economic growth was very modest at best.

Production from the land is in the end dependent on the production of people, so that the fertility of man and woman intervenes within the tie between man and soil. It is no coincidence that as Adam and his Woman are about go out from the Garden at Yahweh's command, the Yahwists relate that Adam gave her a name:

> And the *Adam* called his wife's name Life-maker (*Ḥavah*) because she was the mother of all living (*Ḥay*). (Genesis 3:20)

This wordplay is lost in English, so that the name "Eve" (a poor transliteration of *Ḥavah*) lacks the resonance with "life" that the Hebrew text conveys. Even though the land provides Adam's purpose, Eve gives the life without which land is useless. Unity with a wife, following the principle of realizing that a couple amounts to "one flesh," therefore justifies a man giving up the land of his birth family. Although marriage is grounded in contractual agreement, it becomes a new creation, a remnant of Eden in a world that has all but forgotten that garden of delight.

Marriage by the time of the Yahwists was legal and contractual, working in tandem with the psychological affinity between man and woman that derives from their being "one flesh." The closing verse of Genesis 2, immediately following the creation of Woman, asserts with deceptive ease:

> They were both naked, the Man and his Woman, and they were not ashamed. (Genesis 2:25)

As we've noted, nakedness is often taken as a metonym for sexuality in the Hebrew Bible, and so, in all likelihood, it is here. Sexuality as such is not represented as involved with any sort of curse; that appears later. Just as the work of the garden is instinctive, spontaneous, and rewarding, so relations between man and woman emerge naturally and without shame. That will quickly change; but for the moment, "Eden" has lived up the meaning of "pleasure." The issue of bearing children has not even been raised, so that Adam will not refer to the woman as Eve until after she has received Yahweh's rebuke for heeding the Serpent and consuming forbidden fruit.

When shame does appear, that happens brutally. As soon as the fruit is consumed, both Man and Woman see that they are naked and cover themselves (Genesis 3:8). Their actions are the instinctive result of the self-consciousness and a physical sensation of being reduced in status. Shame is the opposite of honor, which was the social capital of life in the Iron Age society of Israel. Failure in the work of the fields, failure to fulfil an obligation to another person, failure to defend one's family—these failures were deeply humiliating and came with a visceral reaction. Strangely, without anyone seeming to wish it to be so, nakedness and sexuality also became shameful, so that people came to associate intimacy, which had been unself-conscious, with the possibility of humiliation. Tainted with the fear that sexuality might bring dishonor, sexuality introduced a desire to dominate into human relations from which humanity has not recovered.

As we move from Genesis chapter two into chapter three, we shift out of unashamed territory into ashamed territory, with the eating of the fruit. As we've already discussed, what really angered Yahweh was Adam's attempt to excuse his action by saying, "The Woman you gave me, alongside me, she gave me from the tree, and I ate." Eve makes a similar excuse: "The snake misled me and so I ate" (Genesis 3:12–13). And this is what brings about Yahweh's punishment. At first sight, its terms of reference are inexplicable. Yahweh says, "I shall increase your labor and your pregnancy" (Genesis 3:16).

Childbearing becomes the issue, but here it is presented as labor, which is same word used in relation to the curse given to Adam by Yahweh—that is, he's going to have to farm the earth with labor. She has to labor to bring forth the flesh and blood from which she herself is made. And at the same time, the implication is that her pregnancy is lengthened. Clearly, the conception of the Hebrew is that it takes longer for a woman to gestate than other animals (which, of course, is both true and untrue, depending on the animal).

Yahweh is not through. He continues (again, Genesis 3:16): "Your longing shall be for your man and he will rule over you." Notice the text does not say (although later texts do) that men were produced first and then women, and that therefore men rule over women. What the text does say is that there is going to be a change in Eve's longing, which results in the ability of a man to dominate her.

The slide into this change is set by Adam's dreadful example of blaming "the Woman" given to him by Yahweh for introducing him to the fruit. She also passes the blame, by saying, "The Serpent misled me, and so I ate" (Genesis 3:12-13). Within the Yahwists' epic, the habit of attempting to conceal responsibility from Yahweh is what most enrages him, and Eve suffers as a result. In considering Adam in the last chapter, we noticed the contrast with David, who admitted to an egregious sin and was forgiven. Both Adam and now Eve are more like David's predecessor as king, Saul. He broke Yahweh's command while pretending he did not, with the result that the kingship was removed from him and his family and given to David and his dynasty (1 Samuel 15:10–29). The Yahwists understood that, before there was any covenant with Abraham, before the commandments were given to Moses, before the kingdom of Israel was established in David's hand, and indeed before any relationship with Yahweh is conceivable, trust endures as the necessary condition. The word most often translated as "faith" in Hebrew, 'emûnah, in its most fundamental sense means "trust." The word refers to the grounding, mutual confidence that enables people to maintain loyalty to Yahweh, and he with them. Breaking that trust breaks the spontaneous reciprocity that made life in the Garden idyllic.

The "labor" of bearing children Eve is afflicted with corresponds to Adam's labor (Genesis 3:16, 17) in bringing sustenance from the soil. In both cases, what was once intuitive becomes painful for each person within their respective worlds, whether the world of the earth or of flesh. Embedded within Eve's punishment is the all-too-familiar experience of the Yahwists and their community: the often-lethal consequences of childbirth.

Eve's longing for her "man," another facet of her new condition, results in his "ruling over" her, (Genesis 3:16). The word for longing in Hebrew is *teshûqah*, which refers to an impulse of attachment, which makes a person desire something outside as if that thing could suffice to complete an inner sense of lack. In this case, the Yahwists articulate a psychological insight by means of a seemingly naive narrative.

The impulse is not part of Eve's original creation: it is caused by the eating of the fruit. The longing that will come and the desire that led to eating of the fruit commingle in the description of what made her reach out for the fruit:

> The Woman saw that the tree was good for food
> and that it was a delight to the eyes and desirable
> to enlighten; she took from its fruit and ate and
> gave to her man, and he ate. (Genesis 3:6)

In this case, seeing involves much more than sight. In fact, the Serpent has already told her that Yahweh prohibits eating from the tree only because he knows that when she and her man eat it, their eyes will be opened (Genesis 3:5). Even before the fateful punishments from Yahweh that are about to come, when "opened" eyes will discover shame rather delight. What Eve sees that draws her to pick fruit from the tree is an amalgam of what her eyes tell her and the Serpent's promise that she and Adam can "be like gods, knowing good and evil" (Genesis 3:5). Those words and her senses entice Eve: what she hears and sees become completely entangled. Her desire reflects the Yahwists' view of how emotions pull us. The seeing of an object is absorbed into desires projected onto the object, and desire becomes a force that leads and controls our behavior. A sensation, a desire, or an aspiration may be good in itself, but when they are conflated, the narrative warns, the result is a disorientation that in this instance is catastrophic.

In the case of Eve, she sees something that attracts her and surmises that the Serpent must be right in saying that eating it would bring enlightenment. She has heard, she says to the Serpent, that God, while generally permitting fruit to be eaten, has prohibited not only eating from the tree in the midst of the garden but also touching it (Genesis 3:3), a prohibition that Yahweh did not declare to Adam (Genesis 2:16–17). When she did touch the tree to take its fruit, contrary to what she had understood, that action produced no bad result. So why would she not also eat, and give what she ate to her man? Only then, with the forbidden fruit in their bellies, were their eyes opened; with their newfound self-consciousness came an awareness of shame in their nakedness (Genesis 3:7). It marked a division. Before, there had been wholeness and unity, a lack of separation. After they ate, they became not gods but strangers to one another and to Yahweh.

The impulse that had prompted her to take the fruit would in future become a longing directed to her man. She would forever be seeking to go back to Eden, before childbirth brought suffering and the forbidden fruit brought shame—before her longing produced submission. Her subservience, in the Yahwists' view, was of her own making.

How different the primordially feminine appears in the Priestly source, where both male and female are created in God's image and both are blessed by God rather than blighted. Both sources, in their different ways, portray humanity as being in between the animal world and divinity. But beyond that, their two visions of the feminine diverge: one an archetype of positive, embodied empowerment; the other of a knowledge that brings shame, struggle, and curses. By bringing these view together perhaps the redactors' take on our human story is that we need both, which is why both versions of the story are left in the text, existing side by side.

Both visions are still with us. They have wound up, it seems, in our cultural DNA. And today, the dominance accorded to human beings over nature is the source of much criticism of the Priestly source, as is the Yahwists' picture of the dominance of man over woman. Both seem equally arcane and equally unacceptable; and both, in their ways, seem equally incisive.

The Yahwist saga of the first couple, with all its drama and detail, shapes the discussion of gender to this day. What if the Priestly compilers of the Bible had let the first chapter of Genesis stand and then gone on to list the generations that came from the first couple and their progeny, which is, indeed, what happens in Genesis chapter 5? Think of the difference in the contours of our inner world! Eve stands at the center of the Yahwist account. The figure of wisdom she presents is deeply ambivalent. Yes, she is the giver of life, the mother of us all, but with what cost? She will be forever stretching out her hand to pick the fruit, eating of it and offering it to Adam. And to us.

NOTE:

Discussion of the fate of Eve in the treatment of Western interpretation is made accessible in Elaine Pagels, *Adam, Eve, and the Serpent* (New York: Vintage Books, 1988) and Shelly Colette, "Eroticizing Eve: A Narrative Analysis of Eve Images in Fashion Magazine Advertising," *Journal of Feminist Studies in Religion* 31.2 (2015), 5–24.

3.

Abel
New Promise

**At the end of days Cain brought an offering to Yahweh
from the yield of the earth; Abel also brought,
from the firstborn of his flock and their fat. Yahweh
looked to Abel and to his offering, but to Cain and his
offering he did not look.** GENESIS 4:3–5a

THE STORY OF Eden starts, stops, and restarts. Adam
and Eve's expulsion from the Garden seems to bring the
narrative to a close, but then Eve gives birth to Cain and
Abel (Genesis 4:1–2). She indeed becomes "the mother of
all living" (Genesis 3:20). Although the Garden has been
left behind, the Yahwists still depict a primordial existence
in a kind of penumbra east of Eden (Genesis 3:24) in the
Outerworld, which is neither here nor there, a kind of

midway, intermediary zone between Eden itself and the rest of the world.

East of Eden, the firstborn son Cain tills the ground, as his father had been directed to do, while Abel, the second-born, tends a flock (Genesis 4:2). The passage of time is not mentioned, and I think that is deliberate. Life, while not as perfectly seamless and effortless as it once was in Eden before the eating of the forbidden fruit, is still relatively idyllic. It is a world of labor, but also of reward and fullness. At this stage, people (and indeed the whole animal kingdom) are understood to be herbivores (Genesis 1:29-30). The Yahwists in no way contradict that emphatic statement, made within the Priestly source. Flocks are not yet tended for people to consume meat, and meat will not be consumed until the time of Noah within the narrative arc of Genesis (9:3). Sheep gave milk, which could be made into cheese, and provided wool that was used for blankets and clothing. Abel's flock stands for an enhancement of life: the promise that people, despite their transgressions, can live happily after all.

And yet this timeless equilibrium is transitory, almost ephemeral. Abel barely appears in the story, and then he is gone, murdered by Cain. He makes his enduring mark in our imaginations by means of only a few brief verses in Genesis chapter 4. Both Cain and Abel are described as birthed by Eve, with mention of Adam's intercourse with his wife, but with the emphasis on Eve. She calls attention to this herself by giving her first son the name of Cain (*Qayin*), because, she says, "I have acquired (*qaniyti*) a man with Yahweh" (Genesis 4:1). Here, she takes on the role of naming, which before this had been Adam's alone, marking her centrality to birth and framing her role as forming a partnership with Yahweh.

Eve does not give her son Abel a name, as she did in the case of Cain, but he defines himself by what he does, in what immediately follows the naming of Cain:

> And again she bore his brother Abel, and Abel was
> a keeper of sheep and Cain was a worker of the
> soil. (Genesis 4:2)

This role of shepherd alters the norm that had been assigned to males by Adam's creation. Adam had been made from the earth in order to till the earth, and that function is also Cain's. Abel's deviation echoes Eve's creation from flesh rather than the earth. Like Eve, Abel offers life beyond subsidence; they are both more thoroughly social beings than Adam and Cain. Cain is like his father; his life is in the ground. Eve is made from flesh and bone, unlike any other creature; her son Abel likewise breaks precedent, setting out in a new role. Because his activity of tending flocks is new, it is also seemingly untouched by the punishment for disobedience in Eden.

Abel understands the ways of animals and knows what is required for their nurture and continuation. Shepherding is an activity that the Bible will deploy as a metaphor to explain the significance and role of David (1 Samuel 17:34–37), of Jesus (John 10:11–18), and of God himself (Psalm 23), emphasizing the shepherd's protective oversight and guidance.

The first family goes about their lives in the Outerworld. Cain and Abel are productive. But their productivity was different, and that difference became deadly, the Yahwists say, at a specific moment:

> At the end of days Cain brought an offering to
> Yahweh from the yield of the earth; Abel also
> brought, from the firstborn of his flock and their
> fat. Yahweh looked to Abel and to his offering,
> but to Cain and his offering he did not look.
> (Genesis 4:3–5a)

In a narrative that generally lets time go by without notice, reference to this moment as "at the end of days" is startling. The "end" (*qêtz*) might be thought of as the close of the agricultural cycle at harvest time, and there might be a deliberate play on the similar word for "summer" (*qayitz*).

In fact, the prophet Amos used the pun between "summer" and "end" to say that what looked like a sign of summer was in reality of sign of the final judgment coming upon all Israel (Amos 8:1–2). That end was eschatological, concluding all that has to do with temporality with God's definitive intervention. So the phrase "end of days" in Genesis comes across as deliberately ambivalent, as though the action is happening in the past and the future simultaneously. The Yahwists and those who listened to their story knew very well that the plot was approaching the first human death, and the first murder, within human experience as a whole, an event so portentous that it infected all time, primordial, present, and eschatological.

Yahweh's clear preference for a lamb sacrifice reflects the ritual world of the Yahwists, and ancient Israel as a whole, in which animal offerings were seen as the most valuable, and the dearest to Yahweh. As a result, the flock of Abel is a source of sacrifice to God even before it is a source of food for people. Obviously, the pleasure Yahweh takes in the firstborn of the flock produces an angry response from Cain (Genesis 4:5–6), and that response will drive the story. Because cause and effect rivalry follow so closely together in the narrative, we tend to overlook the nature of Abel's offering, which is vital component of the Yahwists' presentation in and of itself.

The Yahwists refer to offerings in sacrifice as a matter of

course because at the time of composition sacrificial practice was routine within Israel, as it was within Near Eastern cultures as a whole. Sacrifice was linked to celebrating the harvest: barley in the spring, wheat in summer, grapes and other fruits in the autumn. People believed that their gods were responsible for fertility, and they included their gods in the enjoyment of fertility's rewards. The form that sacrifice took emerged from the celebration of communal meals, although because in the imagination of the Yahwists animals are not yet used as a routine source of food, in their narrative the link between meals and sacrifice is obscured. Instead, they present sacrifice as Abel's aim, quite apart from providing his community with meat.

In Israel during the tenth century BCE, when the Yahwists were composing their work, the people who brought offerings also shared the offerings. Every product, every animal was prepared as if for a meal, and most of the sacrifice was consumed by worshippers. Some parts of the animal, such as the "fat" specified in Genesis 4:4, were left on the fire and went up in flames; Yahweh was understood to be present as this was happening, hovering over the sacrificial fire and savoring the aroma of the sizzling flesh. The Hebrew Bible links God's pleasure to specific characteristics of offering, especially aroma. When Noah offered sacrifice with the clean animals and birds he had brought with him on the ark, God smelled the pleasing odor, and promised never again to inflict the destruction that he had caused with the Flood (Genesis 8:20-22). Sometimes, sacrifice is a beacon for Israel. In Exodus, as Moses led the people toward the promised land from Egypt, a pillar of cloud showed the way by day and a pillar of fire by night (Exodus 13:21-22). That is exactly what the huge sacrificial fire that burned night and day in the Temple in Jerusalem looked like.

In the Book of Leviticus, a priests' manual for the First Temple built by Solomon, animal offerings are not simply put directly on the flames of the altar; rather, each is butchered, as one would prepare meat for cooking. This is careful work, and the priest amounts to a sacred butcher. Even in the case of the sacrifice called an *ôlah*, which was entirely consigned to the flames, the animal was first slaughtered, bled, and carved up as if for feasting. The concept of the *ôlah* (which means a "going up") was that the whole would be offered as an aroma for Yahweh's pleasure, while most offerings were considered a *zebach shelamim* (a "sacrifice of sharings"). Abel's primordial offering could be of either kind, and the Yahwists might well avoid detail in order to provide a precedent for both types. The Yahwists vital concern was to portray Abel as offering what most pleases Yahweh.

That enjoyment, however, is broken in Genesis, as Abel's action produces just the reaction from Yahweh that sacrifice aims for, yet as a consequence also provokes Cain to murder. By means of narrative, the Yahwists address the dark side of sacrifice. Offerings of the kind and scale that were established during the kingdom of Solomon required a broad, national undertaking. There was a considerable investment in sheep, goats, oxen, doves, various kinds of grain, oil, and wine brought to the Temple for sacrifice. Taxes saw to the upkeep of the priests who handled the construction and maintenance the elaborate Temple buildings. The oversight of this huge undertaking involved the king, but also priests and prophets, among whom controversy often broke out. In the case of sacrifice, many decisions brought significant economic consequences, as well as changes in status among those who were included in or excluded from the operation. Much later, both Judaism and Christianity would see so many problems involved that they came to criticize sacrificial worship and insist that any offering God required was really only metaphorical. For the Yahwists, however, sacrifice was a literal undertaking, no less valuable for all the jealousies and resentments it might produce. The fact that there were winners and losers did not mean the game could be abandoned, because it was the most important game: the contest to please Yahweh. In Abel and Cain, the Yahwists portrayed the dynamics of their own competitive culture.

The drama unfolds from innocence, as is typical of the

beginning actions in Eden and near Eden. Abel's achievement, of discovering the sacrifice that most pleases Yahweh, is not described as deliberate; part of the pleasure in the act is the feeling of instinctive actions and responses, a natural reciprocity and effortlessness. Cain's reaction, however, has nothing to do with pleasure:

> Cain was extremely angry, and his face fell.
> (Genesis 4:5b)

Some negative response seems natural on Cain's part; we can understand his jealousy and hurt feelings. His brother's offering is acknowledged and approved, while Cain's offering is ignored. This natural resentment will decay silently, rapidly, and violently into fratricide, all because Yahweh seems to midjudge the situation.

Yahweh registers Cain's response, and it might seem that Yahweh wants to be helpful. But what he says to Cain only stokes the elder brother's anger:

> Yahweh said to Cain, "Why are you angry, and why has your face fallen? If you do good, isn't there acceptance? And if you do not do good, a sin-offering lies at the door: its longing is for you, and you shall rule over it!" (Genesis 4:6–7)

Within the world of sacrificial practice that the Yahwist inhabited, this is simply an example of practical advice. It seems cryptic at first reading because we no longer inhabit that world, but we can enter into its universe of values and practices.

Because most sacrifices involved communal celebration, people joined in by partaking themselves of the offerings, although part—especially the aromatic fat as well as blood, the very principle of life (Genesis 9:4)—belonged to Yahweh alone. In the case of a sin-offering, however, the person bringing the sacrifice does not partake of the flesh: that is left for others, so that this offering compensates for some wrong that has been done. Once a sin-offering has been effective, the originating sin is not a lurking stain but is simply wiped out; Leviticus 4:1–6:7 details this procedure. So in this case, Yahweh tells Cain that in the ordinary course of his life Yahweh appreciates him, and if in some case he does not do as he should, a sacrifice for sin is always available, from any animal in Abel's flock that Cain might find near the door of his dwelling.

The compressed language of Genesis has led to misunderstanding in the past. The word for "sin" is the same as the word for "sin-offering" *(ḥaṭa' at)* so that some translations stray from the context of sacrifice and imagine that Cain is told to engage in some sort of metaphysical combat with sin itself. That is very far from the practical, direct world of the Yahwists. Sheep are indeed sufficiently compliant to enable people to do with them as they will, and since they are Yahweh's preferred sacrifice, they are ideal as sin-offerings.

The way Yahweh speaks of the compliance of sheep is evocative. When he says, "Its longing is for you and you shall rule over it" (Genesis 4:7), that echoes his statement to Eve, whose "longing will be for your man, and he shall rule over you" (Genesis 3:16). The similarity in language is far too close to be coincidental. Rather, the sense of the Yahwist is that that longing or desire has a connection to being ruled or put under submission. Just as Eve fell under the spell of the beautiful fruit and was punished by having her desire fixated on her husband, so domesticated animals are subservient to human masters, whom they desire to please. The language is simple, but it is also very carefully chosen. Hierarchy in the mind of the Yahwist is not simply an imposition of power but also a consequence of people and animals longing for endorsement and security from a higher authority. In the case of a sin-offering, that means the sheep can readily be led to its slaughter.

What Yahweh has said to Cain simply reinforces the divine preference for Abel's offering. This is not only a matter of a single event, but reaches into the entire sacrificial system of Israel, whether the purpose is communal celebration, the worship of Yahweh, or reconciliation after sinful conduct. All ritual leads back to Yahweh's preference for the flock rather than the produce of the field.

Yahweh's preference for Abel's offering may seem to be harmless favoritism, but its result is that Cain, the first of the brothers to be born, is repeatedly put in the second position: first in the sacrifice Yahweh prefers, and then in the specification that Abel's flock is the source of any sin-offering. Abel stands for the whole system of sacrifice, which marginalizes Cain's status as an outsider on the edge of the system. Yahweh has not seen beyond his own preference, pushing Cain to fury. The idyll of productive work and cooperation of life east of Eden is crumbling before our eyes.

Without preamble or explanation, far darker behavior than anything described so far in Genesis seizes the story line:

> Cain spoke to Abel his brother, and when they
> were in the field, Cain arose against Abel his
> brother and killed him. (Genesis 4:8)

Genesis makes no reference to the murder weapon or exactly how the murder was committed. Unlike the story of the disobedience of Adam and Eve, no explanation is provided of why what Cain has done is wrong. To the Yahwists, murder is an irreversible and obviously egregious act.

Shedding blood is Yahweh's prerogative. The later story of the covenant with Noah, with its account of a sacrifice on behalf of humanity (Genesis 8:20–22) helps us to understand the sense and value of Abel's sacrifice. What God says to Noah also specifies why Cain's murder is incompatible with worshipping Yahweh:

> Indeed flesh with its life—its blood—you shall
> not eat. Indeed for your blood, for your lives, I
> will demand reckoning, from every beast I will
> demand reckoning and from people: from any
> brother of a man I will demand reckoning of the
> person's life. (Genesis 9:4–5)

Blood is the province of Yahweh—killing is a crime against both God and humanity.

Cain does not grasp the full gravity of his act, but he does realize he has done wrong. He attempts to hide the deed, much as Adam and Eve had attempt to elude Yahweh after they had eaten from the Knowledge tree. Cain claims not to know where Abel is when Yahweh enquires about him. He fatefully asks, "Am *I* my brother's keeper?" (Genesis 4:9). Cain intends the rhetorical question to deflect responsibility, but he also asks it in a very specific way in order to attribute responsibility to Yahweh. In Hebrew, he asks "Am *I* my brother's keeper?" because the use of the pronoun for

"I" makes for emphasis (*hashomer 'aḥiy 'anochiy?*). In context, the question implies that it is and always was Yahweh's task to care for his creatures, not Cain's.

By his response Cain has therefore repeated the attempt to shirk responsibility that Adam and Eve exemplified in the garden and has compounded that with his gambit of implicitly portraying Yahweh as liable for an act that Cain himself committed. Yahweh's response reflects his awareness that this is the greatest wrong he has encountered: "What have you done? The sound of your brother's blood shouts to me from the ground" (Genesis 4:10). Yahweh has already said that the ground would be cursed for Adam's transgression (Genesis 3:17). So now the ground, again responsive to Yahweh, shouts out the offense Cain committed, and then compounded with his lie.

Yahweh curses Cain from the ground altogether, so that not even hard work will produce results that will ensure survival:

> Now you are cursed from the ground that opened its mouth to receive your brother's blood from your hand; when you work the ground it will not give you its strength. You will be a fugitive and wanderer on the earth. (Genesis 4:11–12)

From the perspective of the Yahwists, whose work was

composed as the people of Israel entered into sequential struggles to secure a place in a land then called Canaan, the natural work of a man was in the field, with the soil. Cities to Israelites were not centers of civilization, but obstacles. They remembered places such as Jericho, Ai, and Hazor as mortal enemies that needed to be defeated, centers of idolatry and oppression. Only with the close of the period of the composition of the Yahwist source did one city offer an exception to the rule, when David conquered and took the city of Jerusalem as his own.

That exception aside, the corruption of cities was evident to the Israelites who entered the land of Canaan. Each city was not only an obstacle to settlement but also a powerful military reality that threatened the subsistence agriculture which Yahweh had promised would prosper when they were liberated from Egypt. The superior power of the Canaanite lords went hand in hand with their worship of gods and goddesses apart from Yahweh, practices of sexuality that did not correspond to the law of Moses, and even dietary habits that broke the Torah's regulations of purity. This deep and immediate antipathy to the very notion of a city makes one of the achievements of the Yahwists all the more impressive: they argued successfully for Jerusalem as the single exception to the rule that cities were corrupt. Here, in this city and this city alone, protected by the dynasty of David, Yahweh watched over his people. At the time that Solomon built the Temple, this assurance endorsed his work:

> The word of Yahweh came to Solomon: As for this Temple you are building, if you follow my decrees, execute my judgments and keep all my commands, to obey them, I will establish my word through you, which I spoke to David your father. And I will live among the Israelites and will not abandon my people Israel." (1 Kings 6:11–13)

In order to portray Jerusalem as the unique exception to the urban norm, the Yahwists portrayed Cain, the first murderer, as the progenitor of cities generally.

The name "Cain" derives from a verb meaning "smith" in many ancient Semitic languages. The city is a place of metal working and other crafts, which Genesis attributes to the progeny of Cain along with the foundation of the first city (Genesis 4:17–24). The nature of cities and their negative evaluation by the Yahwist will take up our attention further as we move through the text because they are connected with the character of Cain in the Yahwists' imagination.

Abel stands above urban pollution, the ideal of what Israel should become. He is emblematic of keeping sheep, moving from pasture to pasture, and farming when occasion permits as herds are moved from one place to another. The most distinctive aspect of this itinerant, seminomadic life is that it supports herds. Sheep are an enormous burden on the environment, so that remaining in one place is not sustainable. Over the course of a year, hundreds of miles will be covered; sowing and harvesting are timed to take place as flocks are moved through a given area. Israelites typified this pattern of transhumance nomadism, following a circuit that involved sophisticated calculations. There is nothing aimless or haphazard about gauging an itinerary on the basis of weather, the growth rates of crops, and the presence or absence of enemies and predators.

Abel stands for this kind of expertise; as a shepherd, he's able to manage all the variables in this way of life and prosper. He was indeed Yahweh's favorite, but his passage in Genesis is so brief that he is elusive. Unlike Adam, Eve, and Cain, Genesis does not provide the etymology of Abel's name. In Hebrew, however, the term *Hevel* can mean "vapor" or—as is the case here—"breath"; he both breathed life into the image of a good shepherd and, at Cain's hand, disappeared like a breath of wind. Yet alongside the remembrance of Yahweh's pleasure in just the kind of sacrifice that Abel pioneered, every pasture is a reminder of a person once who, without any command to do so, found a new activity that lifted his companions out of subsistence, inventing a way of life to sustain the herds he established and kept. Like much else from Eden, Abel's archetypal endeavor has survived long beyond his death. His fleeting appearance holds out the prospect that his activity can be taken up by Israel.

NOTE:

The literary artistry of the Yahwists is explored in Karolien Vermeulen, "Mind the Gap: Ambiguity in the Story of Cain and Abel," *Journal of Biblical Literature* 133.1 (2014), 29–42. Results in later interpretation are targeted in John Byron, "Abel's Blood and the Ongoing Cry for Vengeance," *The Catholic Biblical Quarterly* 73.4 (2011), 743–56.

4.

Cain
The First Murder, the First City

Yahweh said to Cain, "Where is Abel your brother?"
He said, "I do not know; am *I* my brother's
keeper?" GENESIS 4:9

ABEL'S PLACE IN the Yahwists' account is both powerful and spare. He stands for the last remnant of the Edenic idyll, the shepherd-son who instinctively pleases Yahweh, the prototype of a way of life that would sustain the Israelites from the Exodus through the founding of the Temple, where the sacrifice of animals was especially prized. He is indeed the progenitor of the practice of meat sacrifice that the Temple prioritized. By the time of the Yahwists, a vast operation, ensuring that thousands of animals could be slaughtered, butchered, and offered on the altar during a single day to sustain sacrifice on a national scale, had been designed and executed. Solomon himself, at the dedication of the Temple, is described as commanding 22,000 oxen and 120,000 sheep to be sacrificed. He directed what was both a huge feast for those who took part (1 Kings 8:62–65) and an assurance that, as he says, "Yahweh our God shall be with us" (1 Kings 8:57).

Abel's death at Cain's hands carries dreadful results for Cain himself and his progeny, and his motivation and character are part of the complex insights inscribed by the Yahwists in this extraordinarily compressed and profound narrative of not only the first murder but also the first death.

The Yahwists address the question of why Cain acted as he did, resulting in the first murder, by speaking of his human motivation. Yet as they do so, their explanation, plausible to be begin with, only takes us so far. We can understand Cain's hurt and jealousy, but fratricide seems wanton and arbitrary, far out of proportion to the hurt he felt. That is because, alongside Cain's psychology, the Yahwists also pursue a narrative exigency. The arc of their epic must take us from us from the quasi-idyll of Abel in the Outerworld to the real world of their time. Cain plays a pivotal role in that transition because his actions result in the foundation of cities. Generations will unfold before cities will spread and develop into empires, before Abraham will be called out of a city to the east to obey the command of Yahweh, before Moses will bring Israel out of imperial Egypt, and before David will at last claim Jerusalem as his own. The Yahwists foresee all this as they tell the story of Cain, whose character becomes far more complex than the immediate requirements of the plot demand, because he is implicated in the deeply ambivalent image of the city.

In his offering to God, Cain had every reason to expect Yahweh's approval. He successfully worked the ground (Genesis 4:2) that had been cursed as a result of Adam's disobedience (Genesis 3:17-19), not his own. Yahweh had promised thorns, thistles, and hard earth, but Cain coaxed production from the land. Even after the curse, then, Cain maintained the purpose of Yahweh in creating Adam to till the ground (Genesis 2:5). There is a strong sense of perseverance in his actions, which proves an enduring and positive trait.

For that reason, Yahweh's preference for Abel's offering from the flock is not merely arbitrary from Cain's point of view: it demeans his own considerable effort. Yahweh's failure to understand why Cain was "angry and his face fell" (4:5b-6) not only shows a lack of imagination but also an absence of ordinary human feeling. In contrast, Cain's feelings boil over.

The poetic narrative of the Yahwists usually does not rely on explicit language to convey emotions. Instead, a laconic, deliberately understated description of actions is the rule. So it is with the pivotal event of Genesis chapter 4. Cain speaks to Abel when they are alone in the field, and "Cain arose against Abel his brother and killed him" (Genesis 4:8). Disappointment, jealousy, wrath are not mentioned, and yet they cry from the text as plainly as Yahweh says that Abel's blood shouts to him from the ground (Genesis 4:10). In saying that, Yahweh implies that bloodshed was the means of death: Cain has acted in his rage, presumably using a weapon, an edged rock if not a knife, to eliminate his brother.

Because elimination is the aim, Cain's response when Yahweh asks him where is brother is laden with irony: As we've noted, Yahweh said to Cain, "Where is Abel your brother?" He said, "I do not know; am *I* my brother's keeper?" (Genesis 4:9). Cain's caustic response challenges Yahweh. Isn't it Yahweh's role and responsibility to look after his creation? And why did Yahweh add insult to injury, further provoking Cain's anger and jealously, by telling Cain that he could always use one of Abel's sheep to please God in a way he himself could not (Genesis 4:7)? Why, Cain implies, is it his job to be his brother's keeper when it is Yahweh who has ordered creation? It's interesting that Cain uses the word "keeper" in relationship to his brother–the word could also be applied to a shepherd and his flocks. Is Cain also suggesting that it is not for him but for Yahweh to take on the role as the shepherd of his people? Yahweh responds to the presence of Abel's blood in the earth with a curse:

> When you till the earth, it will no longer yield its strength for you: you shall be a shiftless wanderer on the earth. (Genesis 4:12)

This curse is worse than Adam's curse: Cain will be left to wander, bereft of access to fertile earth. Cain not only understands the depth of the curse but also feels its gravity viscerally:

> Cain said to Yahweh, "My affliction too big to bear! Look: Today you have expelled me from the face of the earth, and from your face I shall be hidden. I shall be a shiftless wanderer on the earth, meaning that everyone who finds me shall kill me." (Genesis 4:13–14)

In this rich and layered statement, Cain openly expresses his humiliation, pain, and existential fear. The emotions are explicit, an unusual tack for the Yahwists. The self-consciousness of Adam and Eve in the Garden, which caused them to experience shame, in Cain's case becomes the self-consciousness of vulnerability, mortality, and imminent death. He is the first fully reflective human being in the Yahwists' account of human origins, and his self-awareness is expressed by means of a protest at his new condition.

Part of the skill of the Yahwists' presentation is that Cain expresses fear that what he did to Abel will now happen to him: "everyone who finds me shall kill me" (Genesis 4:14). Cain feels that the burden is simply too great. He uses the Hebrew term *'avoniy*, here rendered "my affliction," which refers to guilt and also to the punishment for guilt. "Affliction" conveys both those meanings, while terms used in other renderings, such as "punishment" or "iniquity," speak of either what has brought guilt or of punishment for guilt, but not of both at the same time.

The double reference, to the guilt incurred and to the guilt to be punished, grounds Cain's insight about himself. He has realized his guilt from the moment he killed his brother. Reflecting on that breach takes Cain to the next layer of his lament, which is that Yahweh himself is the force that expels Cain from the earth (Genesis 4:11–12). Because that is Yahweh's doing, Cain is exiled from Yahweh personally just as he is exiled from the earth, because after all it was Yahweh who had put Adam on the earth to till it. Cain has been expelled "from the face" of the earth and will no longer appear "from the face" of Yahweh (Genesis 4:13). That nonappearance is expressed in Hebrew in a way that cannot quite be rendered into English. The phrase here, "I shall be hidden" (*'esatêr*), is constructed in a verbal form called the *niphal* that could also be translated "I shall hide myself." That is, the Hebrew wording expresses Cain's awareness that Yahweh is reacting to his murder of Abel but that he is also exiling *himself* from Yahweh's presence.

Cain's sense of isolation makes him aware of his vulnerability. As a "shiftless wanderer," he complains he will be easy prey for those who would kill him, as he had killed Abel (Genesis 4:14). That sense of being exposed, and also of every stranger as an inevitably deadly threat, will shape his attitude and the attitude of his lineage. Yahweh, in response, prohibits any killing of Cain and signals this prohibition:

> And Yahweh said to him, "Therefore everyone who kills Cain shall have vengeance taken on him seven times." Yahweh put on sign on Cain, so everyone finding him would not strike him. (Genesis 4:15)

The "sign" or "mark" of Cain has provoked speculation along many lines. It was used during the nineteenth century among segregationists to justify racial theories, according to which only a certain sort of people derive from Cain, distinguished by skin color, body shape, and cranial capacity. But the Yahwists derive Lamech from Cain (Genesis 4:18), and Lamech was the father of Noah (Genesis

5:28–29), from whom all human beings are descended. Noah's sons, not Cain, Lamech, or Noah, settle in different parts of the world (Genesis 5:32, and chapter 10). Rather than referring to some physical trait, Cain's sign is likely imagined by the Yahwists as a tattoo or scarring of the face, a practice that was already prevalent before the Neolithic period.

Marked by his protective sign, Cain "went out from before Yahweh," withdrawing from God's presence (Genesis 4:16). He settles in a new land called "Nod," a term that reflects the verb for "wandering" (*nûd*). That language would seem to presage endless, nomadic travel, but Cain's legacy proves more complex in the Yahwists' presentation.

Cain marries and his wife gives birth to Enoch (Genesis 4:17). No mention of where the woman came from, who she was, or her blood relation to Cain appears anywhere in the text. As a result, later interpreters referred to Cain and Abel both being married to their sisters; rivalry for the prettier of the two produced grounds for the first murder in some of these imaginative extensions of the Yahwists' work. As in many other cases, imagination can overwhelm the purpose of the text.

The mystery of Cain's wife is not a defect of the account; rather, the Yahwists use individual characters to represent collective human realities. Adam acts as a distinct person throughout, but those who heard the stories about him originally never forgot that his name is nothing other than the word for "man," *'Adam*, who was fashioned from the earth in order to work the earth (*'Adamah*). Similarly, Eve was "Mother of all living" (Genesis 3:20), a model of the feminine in its uniquely creative character. Abel—the paradigmatic shepherd—bears the name of "breath" both because he brings a breath of life to humanity with a new activity beyond scraping subsistence from the earth and because he and his way of life would be blown away by what Cain represents: the challenge of cities.

To an audience that understood clearly and naturally that the characters are representations of collective realities, and not at all isolated individuals with biographies that made them different from everyone else, it was not at all difficult to imagine other people existing at the same time as the named characters. In modern literature, the distinction between a historical figure and a symbolic figure is usually clear. For this reason, when the characters of Eden and east of Eden are considered, it has been tempting to see them as symbolic, since they are obviously not historical in the usual sense. But using the category of symbol misses a vital aspect of these characters in Genesis. In the narrative of the Yahwists, the characters represent, not only certain human possibilities and aspects of their personalities but also enduring models of human existence itself. In the real world in which the story is told, tilling, bearing children, shepherding, and founding cities are the ongoing realities of life.

Just as the modern conception of a symbol misses the living power of social archetypes that the Yahwists develops, so the ancient conception of myth also does not quite capture the Yahwists' achievement. Mythic explanation was a powerful tool in antiquity, deployed in order to use a story about divine or semidivine figures quite different from ordinary experience in order to account for how people live in the present. So, for example, the Babylonian epic of creation, the *Enuma Elish*, depicted the beginning of the world as a combat, in which the storm god Marduk slew Tiamat, the goddess of primordial chaos, and fashions her body into the heavens and the earth. Different forms of this myth, which appeals to the sense of the world being the result of deep strife, were widespread in the ancient Near East. The Hebrew Bible also reflects the saga, in the belief (quite unlike the nonviolent first chapter of Genesis) that Yahweh himself once wrestled the primordial dragon Leviathan in deadly combat (Psalm 74:12–17).

Myths, like symbols, have their own peculiar power and offer scope for creative invention. But the human actors we have encountered in and around Eden are not merely figures from a primordial past. They are also, in the experience of the Yahwists and their audience, the enduring archetypes that, willingly or not, human beings reflect in their daily existence. In Cain's case, after he leaves the presence of God, he is associated with cities. This comes to expression at the same moment that his wife and son come into the narrative:

> Cain knew his wife—she conceived and brought
> forth Enoch—and he built a city, and he called the
> name of the city by the name of his son Enoch.
> (Genesis 4:17)

A long lineage unfolds after this statement, but the foundation of what follows is the city, which is as distinctive to Cain as shepherding is to Abel. It is what he sets in motion that distinguishes him from Adam and opposes him to the activity of Abel. As Cain killed his brother, so a consequence of the rise of a city is its elimination of pasture lands, which are crucial to the care of a herd.

Jerusalem, we've seen, the center of Israel, is the exception to the rule that cities are destructive. It is the place to which David would bring the ark of the covenant, where Yahweh was enthroned in the Temple and established David's throne (2 Samuel 7). That was possible because David captured the city from its original inhabitants and made it his own capital (2 Samuel 5). It was David's son, Solomon, however, who actually accomplished the building of the Temple, following the oracle of the prophet Nathan to David:

> He shall build a house for my name and I will
> establish the throne of his kingdom forever.
> (2 Samuel 7:13)

The prophecy of permanent Davidic rule became a vital foundation of messianic hope within the literature of Israel, and the corollary of that hope was confidence in Jerusalem as Israel's eternal capital.

It's interesting that both David and Solomon themselves epitomize the pattern of the compromised morals of cities: they both embody the messianic promise and yet fail as human beings. David commits adultery with Bathsheba (2 Samuel 11) and Solomon lapses into idolatry (1 Kings 11:1–8). These are only the most obvious examples of their sins. Yahweh is portrayed as continually disciplining them, and they accept the justice of this punishment.

In the end, therefore, the Yahwists attitude toward cities is ambivalent. Cain, the founder of the city he calls Enoch after his son, does so only because he has lost his place on the ground. He takes a position where, from a secure redoubt, he can appropriate the harvest of the earth that he himself cannot produce. He exemplifies the arrogance of any king, whom the prophet Samuel predicted would inevitably become exploitative:

> This will be the policy the king who will reign over you: he will take your sons for himself and put them with his chariot and horses, and they will run in front of his chariot, make them his commanders of thousands and commanders of fifties, or to plow his ground and reap his harvest, or to make weapons of war and equipment for his chariots. He will take your daughters to be perfumers and cooks and bakers. He will take the best of your fields and vineyards and olive groves and give them to his attendants. He will tithe your grain and your vintage and give it to his officials and attendants. Your male and female servants and the best of your cattle and donkeys he will take for his own use. He will tithe your flocks, and you yourselves will become his slaves. (1 Samuel 8:11–17)

With clear-eyed precision, Samuel analyzes monarchy as a parasitic institution. It does not produce but only appropriates.

The city demands not only to eat what it did not cultivate but also to commandeer personnel for its military campaigns. Those campaigns lie at the center of a city's identity, since it inevitably enters into conflict with surrounding peoples and other cities over the land it appropriates. At a bare minimum, the king must defend the territory he has arrogated to himself; in order to prosper, conquest becomes the persistent goal. Because land devoted to agriculture did not produce much beyond a subsidence living, and the means to enhance harvests were limited, more and more lands needed to be conquered.

David and Solomon themselves did not escape the weaknesses of monarchy. David began his sexual relationship with Bathsheba "in the spring of the year, when kings set off" for battle (2 Samuel 11:1); he, however, let his army do the fighting while he took the wife of one of his own officers during his leisure time in Jerusalem. And Solomon, in addition to the gross idolatry he practiced in Jerusalem (1 Kings 11:1-13), provoked revolt by his recourse to enslaving fellow Israelites (1 Kings 11:26-28). Their successors, who lived after the period of the Yahwists, got up to much worse behavior, including the sacrifice of their own children in the cases of Ahaz (2 Kings 16:1-4; 2 Chronicles 28:1-4) and Manasseh (2 Kings 21:1-9; 2 Chronicles 33:1-9). From the beginning of the period of the monarchy, represented by the Yahwists, until its close (for practical purposes) with the Babylonian exile in 586 BCE, the Davidic dynasty stood for both messianic promise and human depravity. This was the common view of the alliance of prophets, priests, scribes, and poets who first put the Hebrew Bible together. Such kings were, in effect, cast in the mold of Cain.

Yet for all the criticism of kings in the line of David, from the Yahwists to the much later editors of the Bible, the hope for a just, Davidic monarch persisted, and with that hope came the collateral aspiration for a peaceful, powerful, and ethically righteous Jerusalem. If any city might be pleasing to Yahweh when all was said and done, it must be this city. The aspiration for Jerusalem's righteous, prosperous destiny went hand in hand with the recognition that it, like all cities, was founded because Cain had been cursed from the land, and brought his capacity for fratricidal violence with him in his exile from the Outer world and God.

When the Yahwists describe the lineage of Cain, they reflect their deep ambivalence regarding the character of such cities:

Irad was brought forth to Enoch, and Irad brought forth Mehujael, and Mehujael brought forth Methushael, and Methushael brought forth Lamech. Lamech took two wives; the name of the one was Adah and the name of the second was Zillah. Adah brought forth Jabal; he was the father of those who dwell in tents and keep cattle. His brother's name was Jubal; he was the father of all those who play lyre and pipe. Zillah, she brought forth Tubal-cain; he was the forger of all instruments of bronze and iron. The sister of Tubal-cain was Naamah. Lamech said to his wives:

"Adah and Zillah, hear my voice;
You wives of Lamech, heed my saying—
        I have slain a man for my wound,
        A young man for my bruise.
        If Cain is avenged sevenfold,
        Truly Lamech seventy-sevenfold."
(Genesis 4:18–24)

Both Cain's curse and the surprising creativity and resourcefulness that he passed on to cities are reflected in this passage, which illustrates the capacity of what seem to be uninspiring genealogical lists to convey a vision of human society.

The curse at the close of the genealogy is stunning. Lamech magnifies the principle of vengeance that protects Cain. Yahweh promised to avenge seven times over (Genesis 4:15), and Lamech vows retribution at the rate of seventy times seven. A nameless "young man" has wounded or bruised him, and Lamech has killed him in return (Genesis 4:24). The text does not detail who the dead man was or what degree of harm he had done to Lamech; he is a nameless cipher in the poetry of vengeance. Yahweh put in play sevenfold retribution to protect Cain from the harm that could come his way because the punishment of landlessness made him vulnerable. But instead of protection, Lamech exacts an escalating retribution, such that merely harming him will result in death. The policy of a militarized city, where merely harming its interest can be lethal, emerges out of the legacy of Cain. The means for implementing violence on this scale are also guaranteed, because "instruments of bronze and iron," which include forged weapons, are provided after Tubal-cain invented the method for creating them. He shared Cain's name (living up to the meaning of "smith") as well as his blood. Even at their most decadent, however, the Yahwists appreciate that cities offer amenities, including musical instruments and the availability of meat offered by herdsman seeking markets, that those in the countryside can only imagine. Cities are places of both danger and pleasure.

The Yahwists leave the question of the ultimate destiny of cities open. They give guidance for how the inheritance of Cain might be corrected. After speaking of Lamech's vengeful pledge, they narrate how Eve welcomed the birth of Seth, compensation for the death of Abel at Cain's hand (Genesis 4:25). Once Seth's son Enosh was born, that "was the start of calling on the name of Yahweh" (Genesis 4:26).

By construing that same Hebrew phrase differently, some ancient interpreters took the meaning to be that

Yahweh's name was "profaned" from that time. The change involves taking the unusual form of the Hebrew verb *ḥalal*, which means "to become the start," as if it meant "to become polluted." The reasoning was that, after all, Yahweh and people have been engaging with one another since the very beginning of humanity's creation according to Yahwists' account, so they would not need to begin calling upon him. To avoid a contradiction in the text, there arose, as sometimes happens, a desire to change its meaning and in this case the verbal form makes such a change possible. But what is possible is not always recommended: the decision to press for another meaning of the verb *ḥalal* arises from a failure to fully appreciate that the curse of Cain made a profound change in humanity's relationship to Yahweh in the plot traced by the Yahwists. As Cain himself says in Genesis 4:14, his punishment means he is both hidden and hides himself from God. There will be no more easy encounters between humanity and its creator, no more natural intimacy: only appeals and worship—a calling on his name. That is humanity's only recourse now that life has moved so far from Eden and innocence.

Through Cain, the Yahwists investigated human traits that are powerful and ugly. We have all felt Cain's jealousy and resentment, of being second when by rights we should be first, of being rejected by that from which we most crave acceptance. Yes, we are repelled by Cain's murder of Abel.

Yes, it seems an extreme response to a perceived slight. Still, our condemnation is not quite complete.

Cain's concern for his own survival prompts Yahweh to provide the protection of a sevenfold vengeance, but then the progeny of Cain exacerbates the cycle of vengeance, making murder an acceptable response to injury. By the time that Lamech recites his poem in celebration of murder, cities have emerged. Cain stands for the capacity of cities to turn to violence and exact retribution for any breach of their complicated laws. Cities intensify people's proximity to one another, and so increase opportunities for jealousy, resentment, aggression, and vengeance. The Yahwists' audience came to understand that, even in Jerusalem, they needed protection from the inheritance of Cain. His story is a cautionary tale but also contains the recognition that Cain lives in each one of us. He is part of who we are.

NOTES:

The mark of Cain is portrayed as metaphorical, namely as knowledge of Yahweh's protection, in R. W. L. Moberly, "The Mark of Cain: Revealed at Last?" *The Harvard Theological Review* 100.1 (2007), 11–28. Although the argument is skillfully developed, it has not won broad support. A more persuasive analysis of what the Yahwists convey as a metaphor appears in Mari Jørstad, "The Ground That Opened Its Mouth: The Ground's Response to Human Violence in Genesis 4," *Journal of Biblical Literature* 135.4 (2016), 705–15.

5.

The Serpent
Language Unravels Eden

The Serpent said to the woman, "Indeed you shall not die! Rather, God knows that in the day you eat from that your eyes will be opened and you will be as gods knowing good and evil." GENESIS 3:4-5

IN THE YAHWISTS' account of Eden, the Serpent occupies a special place. He is key to the unfolding of the action and yet takes up less space in the narrative than any other character except Abel, a mere five verses (Genesis 3:1, 4-5, 14-15). Later interpretation, of course, identifies the Serpent with a figure that never appears at all in Eden and its vicinity: Satan or the devil. No such great antagonist opposed to God appears anywhere in Genesis, or in the Torah, because the conception of a dualistic opponent to Yahweh, a being of equal or nearly equal metaphysical power to God, comes about only much later.

The Yahwists conceived of serpents not as the prime purveyors of evil but as conveyers of wisdom and even healing. Moses is portrayed as fashioning a serpent from bronze, and Israelites bitten by snakes could be cured by beholding this image. Yahweh commanded Moses:

> Yahweh said to Moses, "Make yourself a fiery serpent (*saraph* in Hebrew) and put it on a standard; and it shall be that anyone bitten will look at it and live." So Moses made a bronze snake and put it on the standard, and it happened that if a snake bit a man, but he looked to the bronze snake, he lived. (Numbers 21:8–9)

Considered a mandate from Yahweh, this talisman came to be housed within the Temple in Jerusalem. Devotion to the object, called Nehushtan, was so intense that it was eventually condemned as idolatrous. King Hezekiah determined to smash it because it drew worship that rightly belonged to Yahweh alone (2 Kings 18:1–4). Still, the image of the snake lifted up by Moses in the wilderness also appears in the Gospel according John, as a symbol of how Jesus, lifted up on the cross, will draw a faith that brings not only healing but eternal life:

Just as Moses lifted up the snake in the wilderness,
so it is necessary for the Son of Man to be lifted
up, so that everyone believing in him shall have
eternal life. (John 3:14-15)

This ambivalent presentation of the bronze serpent, as
both curative and an incentive to idolatry, is helpful in
understanding the conflicted presentation of the Serpent in
Genesis. There, the snake is both knowledgeable and leads
the first couple disastrously astray.

Just as serpents and snakes had a long history of
associations with fertility, life, and healing, the rod of the
god Asclepius is the symbol of medical professions. The
entwined snakes around Hermes' staff, known as the caduceus, are sometimes conflated with the rod of Asclepius,
and symbolize divine knowledge, often in the field of
alchemy. Mercury, Hermes' counterpart in Latin, is also the
name of a crucial substance in alchemy, so that the connection is natural.

The divine aspect of serpents survives in an enduring
image within the Hebrew Bible, the vision of Isaiah in the
Temple. There, the prophet directly sees God on his throne,
attended by what the original text calls *Seraphim*:

In the year that King Uzziah died I saw the Lord:

sitting upon a throne, high and exalted, and his robes filled the Temple. *Seraphim* stood about him, with six wings, six wings each. With two each covered his face, with two each covered his feet, and with two each flew. And each shouted out to the other, "Holy, Holy, Holy: Yahweh of armies, the whole earth is filled with his glory!" (Isaiah 6:1–3)

That term was taken up in later theology to refer to an exalted type of angel, but for Isaiah each of these is a fiery snake, winged and equipped for flight (Isaiah 14:29; 30:6). The throne of God is attended by flaming serpents.

Hebrew culture shared the admiration for serpents' apparent cunning, their ability to shift in an instant from seeming lethargy to rapid action, to slough off their skin and emerge all the more vigorous, and to move with effortless precision to their prey. For all those reasons, however, they were also dangerous. In the account of Moses making a bronze serpent, forged in a fire, the motivation is to counteract bites from serpents that are themselves described as fiery: the biting animals are called (*hanehashim haseraphim*, "fiery snakes" in Numbers 21:6), and Moses is told to make, and goes on to make his own "fiery" (*saraph*) version from bronze (Numbers 21:8–9). To a large extent, serpents are dangerous because they approach unexpectedly, slithering on the ground. Moses' antidote is mounted on a staff, the Hebrew equivalent of the rod of Asclepius or the caduceus of Mercury. In the case of Moses, the deliberate elevation of the bronze serpent makes it more easily visible, and also the visual opposite of the snakes on the ground, truly an antidote.

As soon as the Yahwists said the word "serpent" or "snake" (*nahash*) in Genesis 3:1), those who heard the story knew that a powerful, ambivalent, troubling creature was the reference. Part of the narrative skill of an oral tradition is that characters do not need to be invented completely; rather, they are familiar to those who are listening from many accounts they have heard before. The serpent was already embedded in the mythological landscape of the Ancient Near East, and Israelite culture had already absorbed its mythological associations.

The artistry of the Yahwists is displayed neither by simply repeating a general description of the serpent nor by creating a wholly new figure, but by weaving an ancient myth into their epic account of humanity's origin. To accomplish that, the Yahwists needed to portray the Serpent in a way different from other depictions. Understanding this difference is key to appreciating what they achieved.

The characters encountered so far—Adam, Eve, Cain, and Abel—are representatives of people whom the Yahwists and their hearers encountered as a matter of living reality.

Adam, the man created from earth to till the earth, was reflected in every farmer active in the kingdoms of David, Solomon, and Rehoboam, the kings under whom and for whom the Yahwists worked. The vast majority of male Israelites farmed, so that Adam was not a mythic, superhuman figure, but an archetype reflecting a lived reality. Similarly, Eve's description as "Mother of all living" (Genesis 3:20) applied to every mother. Firstborn Cain would found a city that became the prototype for all cities, and his trade as a smith was characteristic of urban life, just as shepherding flocks in the manner of Abel did not die with him, and sacrifices from the flock remained the form of worship that, according to the Yahwists, God himself preferred.

These people are all archetypes, mirrored in the social realities of the Yahwists. Seeing a farmer in the field, a woman near to giving birth, a blacksmith at the forge, a shepherd with this flock even today awakens in most people a sense of nearness to basic truths of human existence. The Serpent of Genesis is different. He is not an archetype. He is a figure that no longer exists in ordinary experience and is used in the story to explain how the present came to be. In this way, the Serpent's function is similar to the Greek's Prometheus, who gave humanity fire, or Rome's Liber, who provided vineyards, or the Egyptian Osiris, who was raised from the dead to become king of the

Netherworld. The result was that people could enjoy fire and wine and trust their dead to divine protection, without anticipating meeting up with Prometheus, Liber, or Osiris anytime soon. These are mythic figures for that reason; they explain current reality, but at the same time are not part of it. The Yahwists treat the Serpent as a myth in exactly this sense, speaking of a being that no longer exists as it is described but which explains why snakes as we can see them look as they do, as well as how they are treated, and—most crucially—how human beings took the fateful step into self-consciousness and knowledge.

The Yahwists begin their mythmaking when they say:

> The Serpent was smarter than any being of the field that Yahweh God had made. He said to the woman ... (Genesis 3:1)

What he has to say is obviously pivotal, but even prior to his words, who the Serpent is and the very fact that he speaks place him in the realm of myth.

The Serpent is, the Yahwists say, the smartest of the animals. This puts the Serpent in a clearly defined category: the "beings of the field" that Yahweh experimented with making when he decided he would find a partner for Adam (Genesis 2:18-19). Beings of the field (and the birds of the air) were, like Adam, created from the earth. They all stand equivalently with Adam in their creation, and they come from the same ground, although they are made after Adam with the intention of benefiting him. The Serpent is one of a class of beings designed for human companionship. At the outset of his encounter with Eve, he also resembles other animals much more than snakes do now, because he has not yet been condemned to crawl on his belly in order to move. That is a curse that will come to him later; for the moment, the Serpent is the mythological progenitor of snakes. He explains how snakes came to be snakes, without being a snake in the normal sense at all.

What distinguishes the Serpent at this stage is not his form but his intelligence: he is smarter than any other animal. Many translations, anticipating how the encounter with Eve and Adam will go, portray this intelligence as malevolent, so that the Serpent is described as more "crafty" or "cunning" or "sneaky" or "clever" or "shrewd" or "wily" than other creatures. The fact is, however, that the term in Hebrew, *'arûm*, can refer to intelligence in either a positive or a negative way. Within the Book of Proverbs, for example, a person who is *'arûm* is the opposite of a fool (Proverbs 12:23). In the Book of Job, however, the same term refers to people who are, as the saying does, too smart for their own good (Job 5:12). The term "smart" indeed seems to cover the range in English; at the time of the King James Version, "subtle" was used, which worked well within the spoken language of the period but seems opaque in this context to most English speakers today.

Why the Serpent should be unusually smart is not stated, and that suggests that the Yahwists simply take up the ancient mythology of the Serpent's unusual intelligence and apply it within their narrative. The scale of their innovation becomes plain when they have the Serpent speak. Until this point in Genesis, speech has been a restricted activity, limited to Yahweh and Adam. The capacity to speak in the case of Eve emerges in her dialogue with the Serpent. But, of course, the Serpent's ability to enter in the world of language is far more startling than Eve's. No other animal is described in such terms. The Serpent is not only exceptionally intelligent but is also uniquely articulate.

The form of his opening address of Eve has attracted a great deal of comment among scholars and theologians:

> He said to the woman, "Has God really said,
> 'You shall not eat of every tree of the Garden'?"
> (Genesis 3:1b)

Of course, anyone who knows the story that the Yahwists have just recounted will understand that the Serpent's statement is a gross distortion, since God had said to Adam, "You shall indeed eat from every tree of the garden" (Genesis 2:16).

In falsifying Yahweh's position, the Serpent also uses the plural form of "you," as if Yahweh had spoken this command to both Adam and Eve. That, of course, was also not the case: when Yahweh instructed Adam about the Knowledge-tree, neither the Serpent nor Eve had yet been created.

Part of the skill of the Yahwists' narrative is the way it shows us that language can be deceptive. The clear command to Adam is muddled in the Serpent's question to Eve, and the implication is that the distortion is far from innocent. Eve, as a matter of fact, initially rises to the challenge with force and accuracy:

> And the woman said, "From the fruit of the tree of the garden we shall eat." (Genesis 3:2)

She rightly corrects the Serpent about Yahweh's command, referring to trees collectively with the singular term "tree," and does not at first quote Yahweh, whom she had not directly heard. She speaks of what "we" shall do on the basis of an understanding she has with Adam. As she replies to the Serpent, however, she also—and innovatively—refers to "the fruit of the tree," not simply the tree. She shifts attention from the nature of the tree in itself to the fruit on the tree. That will prove to have a fateful outcome as events unfold. At base, though, Eve plays the role of calling positive attention to one of the Yahwists' principle themes, of which the Serpent is the negative example: language can be used to corrupt reality.

Eve's statement, "From the fruit of the tree of the garden we shall eat" (Genesis 3:2), raises the question of the Knowledge-tree in particular. In what she says, the term "tree" is in the singular, but is in the collective sense, and most translators render it as the plural, "trees." Yet by using the singular, her speech more easily makes the transition to a specific tree, the singular tree that is prohibited:

> But from the fruit of the tree that is in the midst of the garden, God said, "You shall not eat it and you shall not touch it, or you shall die." (Genesis 3:3)

As compared with the Serpent's insidious question, Eve's reply remains accurate, but as she shifts from paraphrase to quotation, she moves from a seemingly harmless mistake to an outright fabrication. Having corrected the Serpent's distortion, she falls into distortion herself.

Like the serpent, Eve changes the singular "you" of God's command to Adam (Genesis 2:17) into a plural. That may seem innocuous, but in her case, as in the case of the Serpent, the plural usage treats Yahweh's speech as something that had been heard directly, when in fact it was not. The Serpent was created before Eve, but neither of them was alive to listen in on God's directive to Adam alone. In presenting their mutual mistake in this way, the Yahwists are making a subtle but powerful point.

The Serpent and Eve alike can have heard of Yahweh's command only by means of Adam, and yet they put themselves in the position of directly quoting Yahweh. As a result, their departures from Yahweh's prohibitions amount to distortions, and these distortions push the narrative along to its painful result—curses and expulsion from the Garden. The Serpent's distortion is obvious, and is clearly deliberate: even if formed as a question, his suggestion that Yahweh did not want people to live from the trees of the Garden is absurd on the face of the narrative that has preceded it. Eve's distortion is also fateful, but it is unintentional, and, at first sight, curious.

As she responds to the serpent's question, Eve adds to Yahweh's prohibition, again quoting him directly and falsely, "and you shall not touch it" (Genesis 3:3). Not approaching the knowledge tree might seem a wise precaution, since it was not to be used for food, but Yahweh had not said that to Adam. The Yahwists' audience might have imagined Adam, relating Yahweh's command to Eve, adding such a prohibition, but in any case it is an addition, and has the paradoxical impact of weakening the force of the command: after all, during her discussion with the Serpent, Eve will approach the tree and admire the fruit that her own words call attention to, and touch it, all without suffering any harm whatever. That will seem to support the insistence of the Serpent that eating the fruit will also not be harmful. He will even say that eating it will vastly enhance human stature.

But before turning to the Serpent's final argument, the skill of the Yahwists in explaining how Eve became vulnerable to the Serpent's words needs to be appreciated. Because the Serpent has made a manifestly false statement, she rightly pushes back with the correct assertion that she and Adam may eat of the Garden's trees (Genesis 3:2). The term "fruit" in her response foreshadows her visual delight, which leads her to see the fruit as desirable, to touch and take it, and finally to eat it (Genesis 3:6). That succession is embedded in her character, as explored in the discussion of Eve, but she could not have come to that point unless she had turned Yahweh's prohibition into a mandate against touching as well as eating. Her doing so is not at all a consequence of any desire to deceive but comes of her pushing back against the Serpent's assertion. She insists that she and Adam can eat of every tree but one, and in emphasizing that point she makes the exception stronger than it truly was. Eve mistakenly portrays Yahweh as threatening death for touching the fruit, so that when touching proves innocuous, everything else the Serpent says becomes plausible.

The skill of the Serpent's deceit lies in his distortion

of language; he not only exemplifies distortion in his own statements but also produces distortions when Eve corrects his lie. The Yahwists here warn about the capacity of language to garble memory and to manufacture erroneous perceptions. Their audience knows very well that the Serpent and Eve never spoke with Yahweh personally about the Knowledge tree, but here they are both quoting him with a confident authority whose certainty will prove disastrous. Indeed, the more they claim direct acquaintance with Yahweh's words, intentionally or not, the more wrong they are.

The Yahwists' awareness about the pitfalls of language, and especially pitfalls of language when debate presses a participant to take a position in order to refute rather than to understand, sets the Serpent up to make his final claim:

> The Serpent said to the woman, "Indeed you shall not die! Rather, God knows that in the day you eat from that your eyes will be opened and you will be as gods knowing good and evil." (Genesis 3:4–5)

Here, too, the Serpent distorts the threat of Yahweh to Adam (Genesis 2:17), mimicking the threat "you shall indeed die" and the phrase "in the day," turning it upside down into the promise of a godlike knowledge of good and evil, and the divine stature that goes with such knowledge.

The claim would not have worked without its prelude in the dialogue between Eve and the Serpent, but now she is prompted to look at the fruit, desire it, take and eat it, and give it to Adam (Genesis 3:6). Until this point, the Serpent has proved smart but also deceptive, and so it is now. A later biblical text, the Wisdom of Solomon, reflects on the motivation for his deceit and refers to "the devil's envy" (Wisdom 2:24). The identification of the Serpent as the devil reflects the theology of a time long after the Yahwists, but the envy attributed to him captures the sense of what pushes the Serpent to act as he does. He distorts not only Yahweh's command but also Eve's memory of that command and her perception of the attractiveness of the fruit. Envy corrupts language wherever language is applied.

The results of corruption become plain when, instantaneously after eating the fruit, the eyes of Eve and Adam were "opened." But the result is shame rather than knowledge, the desire to conceal themselves rather than magnified stature (Genesis 3:7–10)—and labor for them both in working the earth and childbirth respectively (Genesis 3:16–19).

Yahweh's punishment of the Serpent is even more immediate and physical:

Yahweh God said to the Serpent, "Because you have done this, you are cursed more than all herded animals and all beings of the field! You shall go on your belly and shall eat dust all the days of your life. I shall put hostility between you and the woman, between your progeny and her progeny: he shall wound your head, and you shall wound his heel!" (Genesis 3:14–15)

The curse in this case is direct. Adam has the land accursed as a result of his deed (Genesis 3:17), and Eve is punished without the result being called a curse (Genesis 3:16). To that extent, the Yahwists deal with the fate of the Serpent as definitive. The Serpent is reduced to its present form, wriggling on the ground and consuming dust. It cannot be a coincidence that, just as the working man, Adam, is fated to return to dust, the Serpent is consigned to eat dust. While Adam will eventually return to the substance he was created from, the snake has literally to taste the reality of his origin and destiny every day of its life. In this regard, the literal snake of ordinary experience is the opposite of the mythological Serpent, in that mortality suffuses every moment of experience. Further, the reflexive and visceral hostility, not only between Eve and the Serpent but also between all Eve's children and every snake that there will ever be, defines existence on both sides. People want to crush the head of any snake they encounter in the experience of the Yahwists, and every snake represents danger.

The Yahwists depict a categorical punishment of the Serpent's deception in only a few sentences because they are able to play the snake of their actual experience against the mythological Serpent of their common Near Eastern culture. They do so to powerful effect, and at the same time they use the exchange with Eve to depict the real power of the Serpent: the capacity of language, especially in the dialectical encounter people in argument, to distort what they know, how they act, and their perceptions of what truly is.

Having accomplished so much, it is unlikely that the Yahwists left two issues, directly related to the Serpent, quite unresolved unless there were a purpose in doing so.

First, the curse at the close of the scene makes clear that the writhing, filthy existence of snakes in the present was not a feature of the Serpent's condition in mythological time. Once, snakes were like other animals, moving on limbs with their bodies off the ground. But that elegant touch, which establishes the Serpent as a mythic figure, does nothing to address the entire premise of the encounter with Eve: the mythological Serpent speaks articulately and convincingly even when his purpose is deception, while snakes do not speak at all. The Yahwists tease at the prospect that people and animals might speak, without exploring it. A later story in the Torah, however, will go on to describe how an ass could speak, in the story of the prophet Balaam, as a result of Yahweh's intervention (Numbers 22:28).

The Serpent was not completely deceptive. He said eating from the Knowledge-tree would open people's eyes (Genesis 3:5), and they were opened (Genesis 3:7). The disappointment came in the result, when their awareness was experienced as shame rather than godlike knowledge. But is the awakening of self-consciousness, which produced shame in its arrival, a permanent state? Might it lead to something much more precious? If it does, if self-conscious knowledge is not a curse at all but a means of transcending oneself, then the Serpent was guilty of exaggeration in this regard but not actual deceit.

Indeed, it turns out that the Serpent's exaggeration is very much like Yahweh's. The Serpent had promised Eve, "In the day you eat from that your eyes will be opened and you will be as gods knowing good and evil" (Genesis 3:5), and even if knowledge eventually results in human benefit, that benefit did not arrive on that day. But then Yahweh had threatened Adam, "in the day you eat from that you shall indeed die" (Genesis 2:17). Adam did not in fact die on the day of eating the fruit.

The Yahwists' narrative inevitably raises questions about Yahweh's capacities to control his own creations and to manage their behavior, and in this case a basic issue of character emerges: did Yahweh know when he threatened

Adam with death for eating from the Knowledge-tree that he would not follow through on his threat? Unresolved difficulties of that sort will take us into the next chapter on Yahweh. Because the Serpent not only mistakes Yahweh's purpose but also distorts his intent by a manipulative use of language, the Yahwists call attention to the contagion of falsehood. Whether misstatements are deliberate, as in the case of the Serpent, or inadvertent, as in the case of Eve, they compound one another and result in disaster. Language, used to conceal rather than to reveal, is camouflage, as when Eve blames the Serpent for what she did, and Adam blames Eve for what he did. In a sense, the silence of the Serpent when confronted with what he has done is his only true statement. By that point in the story, the Yahwists have said what they can say about the contagion of false language.

As they bring home their argument, the Yahwists insist by implicit contrast that language that is truthful might avoid disaster, at least to the extent that it avoids misunderstanding. For all that a great deal is lost as humanity moves progressively east from Eden, the prospect that there can be mutual agreement remains alive, provided the contagion of falsehood is avoided. That is a particular challenge, however, because every one of the characters involved is complex and unpredictable. Yahweh creates for no apparent reason; Adam goes silent just as a word might have saved

him and Eve from breaking Yahweh's single command-
ment; Eve rightly corrects the Serpent, but then falls victim
to her own exaggeration; Abel's resourcefulness somehow
stops short of self-defense; Cain resorts to violence for no
stated reason; and the Serpent himself lies, it seems, for
the sake of lying. None of them can be comprehended
unless language can bring clarity to their dark corners. The
darkest of those corners lie within Yahweh, on whom the
Yahwists focus their most intense attention, purging themselves of the distorting approach of the Serpent, whose
example their narrative permanently rejects.

NOTE:

The allure and dread of the mythic Serpent are explored in Richard B.
Stothers, "Ancient Scientific Basis of the 'Great Serpent' from Historical
Evidence," *Isis*, 95.2 (2004), 220–38. The significance of events within
the culture of the Yahwists is nicely detailed in Ziony Zevit, *What Really
Happened in the Garden of Eden?* (New Haven: Yale University Press,
2013).

6.

Yahweh
Conflicted Creator

Yahweh God said, "Look—Adam has become as one of us, knowing good and evil. Now, so he does not stretch his hand out and take also from the tree of life and eat and live forever..." GENESIS 3:22

AS THE YAHWISTS' approached what it meant to live in relation to God, they thought in terms of personal connection. In the arc of their epic of the people Israel, Yahweh had called Abraham and entered into a covenant or contract with him and his sons Isaac and Jacob; Yahweh had brought Israel out of Egypt, choosing Moses and then Joshua to bring them to the Promised Land and personally chose David and his dynasty to rule Israel.

The Yahwists portrayed Israel's relationship with Yahweh as a matter of survival as the small and relatively recently created nation balanced on the edge of destruction at the hands of the surrounding powers of the ancient Near East. There was no prospect that Israel, even with Yahweh's protection of David and Solomon, would dominate the region. The strength of surrounding empires, above all Egypt to the south and Assyria to the north, meant that Israel's prospects would be limited for the foresee-able future.

Survival at the edge required a resilience, a willingness to improvise, and a readiness to enter combat even at a disadvantage. The story of David and Goliath is emblem-atic of the kind of virtue that the Yahwists valued. Their view of Yahweh mirrored their hero, David: loyal, resource-ful, but also sometimes at the mercy of events rather than exercising total control. It is hard for us to imagine, but I think it is clear that the Yahwists saw their God, like David, as a work in progress—someone willing to learn in order to prevail.

Yahweh would be called upon by the people in worship (Genesis 4:26), but his physical proximity was a thing of the past. Prophets were now necessary to interpret Yahweh's intent; sacrifice was required to maintain the connection that made Israel's survival possible. Although Yahweh was still thought of as a palpable, physical being, he was also remote, a powerful presence hovering over Israel in the heavens.

To understand this presence, the Yahwists told their story from the viewpoint of Eden, when Yahweh did approach people directly and his real character was more obvious. Their intent was to describe the personality of Yahweh in his interactions with the creatures he made when the link between Yahweh and his people began. Yahweh might no longer be visible and he no longer spoke directly, but his character as it was portrayed by Yahwists in Eden remained the same.

The Yahwists' most surprising decision was to compose a narrative in which Yahweh acts as a character in relationship to other characters, so that he changes and develops. The dynamic is not just that Yahweh encounters other beings but that they change him as a result of the encounter. This emphasis confuses us. Our modern conception is that God is abstract, and for that reason Yahweh has to seem strange to us. He physically breaths into Adam's nostrils to make him alive, literally shaping him out of earth (Genesis 2:7). Yahweh then plants a garden for him (Genesis 2:8). He goes on make other creatures, adapting to his realization he shouldn't leave Adam on his own.

When Adam and Eve hide themselves after eating the fruit, Yahweh can't find them until Adam reveals himself, and Yahweh, far from omniscient, only gradually realizes what has happened (Genesis 3:8–11). He panics at the thought that his creatures will get advantage over him, putting into words his apprehension that failing to act will result in disaster:

> Yahweh God said, "Look—Adam has become as one
> of us, knowing good and evil. Now, so he does not
> stretch his hand out and take also from the tree of
> life and eat and live forever…" (Genesis 3:22)

Without even finishing that sentence, Yahweh goes on to expel Adam, and by implication Eve, from the Garden. This pattern of failing to anticipate what people will do, not fully grasping the result of their actions, and then improvising a response is repeated in the case of Cain (Genesis 4:3–12, 15). These features of the narrative are not inadvertent.

The Yahwists' conception of the divine is obviously anthropomorphic: Yahweh physically acts as a person would act, with a body that breathes and walks about. Even more profoundly, Yahweh encounters exactly the kinds of limitations that people do, limitations that bring out character.

Long after the time of the Yahwists, the conception of God became far more philosophical, and the Creator was portrayed as all-knowing, without fault, impassive, powerful in every possible respect. In the first century BCE, the Book of the Wisdom of Solomon, a work that combines

Platonic philosophy with the practice of Judaism, will say that "the Spirit of the Lord has filled the world, and that which holds all things together knows what is said" (Wisdom 1:7). This elegant presentation represents the confluence of ancient Israelite traditions with the teaching of Plato and is an important precedent for the conception of God that is pursued in the New Testament. But the Yahwists cannot be forced into the mold of a view that came much later, and attempting to make them conform to later theologies of Judaism or Christianity only makes their narrative in Genesis impossible to understand.

For the Yahwists, only a personal connection can keep Israel in relation to God. For this reason, they willingly pay the inevitable cost involved in portraying the divine in terms of human character: Yahweh had to be, and evidently was, depicted as both vulnerable and limited, as every person is. Seeing that is only the first step in appreciating the Yahwists' work. They and their audience, as a result of depicting Yahweh in human terms, evolved a vivid portrait of the underlying character of the divine—as vivid as their portraits of Adam, Eve, Abel, and Cain.

For the Yahwists, as we've seen repeatedly, names are not assigned to characters by hazard. Each of the people in the story of Eden takes up a role that corresponds to the name assigned, and Yahweh as a name had both an ancient history and linguistic significance. Linguistically the name

Yahweh has a connection with the verb that means "to be" or "to become" (*hayah*). There is an assonance between the name and the verb in Hebrew that is obviously present whether or not there is an etymological link. Although there might be such a link, the name is so ancient, and so widespread in application to deities in Semitic languages before Hebrew even arose, that its original derivation cannot be known with certainty. Those who were fluent in Hebrew, however, would hear the association with *hayah*, although they would not be able to pin down a specific form of the verb as they used it. If there were such a form, it would mean "he-will-cause-to-be," and that sense, perhaps, influenced the storytellers of Genesis. The "y" sound at the beginning of Yahweh's name corresponds to the future in Hebrew, and the "w" is an intensive form that conveys causation.

Because Yahweh is a name, the way that it is used is the best guide to its meaning, and its sense becomes apparent in that context. At a time long after the Yahwists, this name was held in such reference that it was not pronounced at all in routine speech, in order to avoid slighting the honor owed to God. The view grew over time that the name of God should not be used for a vain, trivial, or selfish pursuit (Exodus 20:7), so one is best advised not to use that name at all. The Mishnah, the foundation document of Rabbinic Judaism from the second century CE, limits usage of this name to the High Priest on the Day of Atonement when he presided in the Temple (Yoma 6:2). The conception was that God's personal name needed to be used then, but that was the only time it could be used. As a result, after the Temple's destruction, there was no legitimate use at all. Protection of the name resulted in substitutes being used, including "Lord," "the Name," and "The Holy One, Blessed be He." Those in Rabbinic tradition became quite strict in that regard, eventually extending the practice to the word "God," so that even it would not be spelled explicitly ("G-d" in English). English Bibles routinely render Yahweh as "Lord." This reflects the convention of writing the name Yahweh with its consonants in the Hebrew Bible, but supplying it with the vowels of "Lord." The practice reflects an honorable desire to refer to God with respect by avoiding direct use of his name.

The trouble with such conventions is that they can impede a basic grasp of how the biblical name Yahweh came to be used in the first place. First off, it appears frequently. Obviously, in the time of the Yahwists (and indeed for a long period after them) reference to God with what was believed to be his personal name was widely practiced. In addition, this name also appears in combination with other terms, which were not replaced the way that "Yahweh" was. For example, the expression "Halleluyah," meaning "praise Yah[weh])," has traveled across languages from Hebrew into

English without most people who use it being aware that it incorporates the ancient name Yahweh. The shortened form, "Yah," appears about fifty times in the Hebrew Bible, compared with 6,800 for "Yahweh." In addition, shortened forms appear as part of people's names, including Moses' mother. She was named "Yokebed" (Exodus 6:20; Numbers 26:59), which combines a shorted form of "Yahweh" with the word for "glory." Other names have absorbed forms of the divine name at the end, including Isaiah (*Yeshayahu*) and Jeremiah (*Yerimiyahu*). Similarly, the word for "God," *'el*, is included in names such as Ezekiel and Daniel. Those familiar with Hebrew might use a variety of means to refer to God circumspectly, but they also were well aware that divine names permeated their culture.

Inclusion of "Yahweh" in naming people supports the understanding that at base Yahweh was a protective deity, a person's heavenly patron. By the time of the Yahwists, the name Yahweh had been known as a tutelary deity of both particular individuals (whose names resonated with Yahweh's name) and of the people of Israel as a collective. The Yahwists extended that concept in their daring narrative. They put their own tutelary deity at the pivotal, opening point of life on earth, by beginning their account, "These are the bringings forth of the heavens and earth, while they were created, in the day Yahweh God made earth and heavens" (Genesis 2:4).

At this time, according to the description in Genesis 2, nothing grew in the earth because there was no rain and no person to till the earth, and Yahweh both made the first person from dust and personally planted the Garden (Genesis 2:8-9). So focal is the concentration on the making of Adam, the Garden is installed without mention of rain, and rain will not be mentioned in the Book of Genesis again until the time of Noah (Genesis 7:4). Fundamentalist readings of the text assert that there really was no rain until the time of Noah, but the luxuriance of the Garden demands that Yahweh had seen to that as well, as is implied in the statement:

> Before, no plant of the field was on the earth and no grass of the field grew, because Yahweh God had not made it rain upon the earth and there was not a man to work the earth. (Genesis 2:5)

The first rain and the first person came together, making the Garden possible.

Genesis indeed is a story of "bringings forth" or "generations," a term that will also be used by the Yahwists to describe how people are brought forth in a sequential, causal pattern. Yahweh is creative: that is the core of his character. He does not create *ex nihilo* ("out of nothing") as in later theology: he makes life from preexisting material.

The Yahwists do not tell their story from a viewpoint in time when there was no matter, and they do not pose the question of how the raw materials of creation became available to Yahweh. Other stories of creation were available during their period, and just as they could easily imagine the existence of people beyond Adam, Eve, and their immediate progeny, so they understood that other deities and different stories of creation were widely acknowledged in the land in which they lived.

Yahweh, however, was Israel's one god, and his character for the Yahwists has to do with creativity in a particular respect: the bringing forth of life. Everything Yahweh does in creation is lavish, even excessive. There is over-abundance in every direction. In producing trees to grow, Yahweh makes "every tree" sprout—all that delight the eye and give food, without limit. In that absence of limitation, he also puts in the midst of the Garden both the Life-tree and the Knowledge-tree (Genesis 2:9). The original audience of the Yahwists, together with today's readers, know what is coming, but before the drama unfolds, the question is inevitable: why are those trees, which might cause trouble and certainly do so eventually, included at all? When Yahweh creates, he does so on a scale that can get out of his control, so that he is forced to intervene in ways he does not intend from the outset.

The first such intervention comes when he instructs

Adam in the ways of the Garden, the fateful passage which the Serpent twists and Eve misconstrues:

> Yahweh God commanded Adam, "You shall
> indeed eat from every tree of the Garden, and from
> the tree of the knowledge of good and evil—you
> shall not eat from it! Because in the day you eat
> from it you shall indeed die." (Genesis 2:16–17)

Although the prohibition of the Knowledge-tree is unequivocal, it is also belated, and interrupts the grand mandate to eat everything. It is as if Yahweh realized only in midsentence that he had to put that particular tree off limits. He does so, but also gives no reason, except that Adam will die immediately from eating the fruit of that tree. The prohibition arises because Yahweh has created on a more lavish scale than needed for his immediate purpose; putting the Knowledge-tree off limits to Adam is less about Adam himself than it is about Yahweh's lack of foresight. Yahweh's creativity gets ahead of his planning. It is as if Yahweh realized after the fact that he and Adam were different, and desired to hold back some of his own creativity from his creation.

In the primal setup of the Garden, then, Yahweh improvises both by prohibition (of the Knowledge-tree) and by inventive creativity (in the case of producing Eve as a companion for Adam) in order to cope with the consequences of his own realizations concerning what he has made. He is not omniscient, but he is constantly resourceful. The Serpent, his own creature, will put his resourcefulness to the test.

When it comes to realizing his own intentions, Yahweh reaches that point only by means of his actions. Unaware of what has happened between the Serpent, Eve, and then Adam, Yahweh walks in the Garden in the pleasant evening breeze and has to ask where Adam and Eve have hidden themselves (Genesis 3:8–10); then what has happened dawns on him, as he confirms with his questions:

> He said, "Who told you you were naked? Have you eaten from the tree I commanded you not to eat from?" (Genesis 3:11)

Once his interrogation is completed (Genesis 3:12–13), Yahweh's verdict is immediate and calibrated to what the Serpent, Eve, and Adam have done.

The calibration is detailed in the same sequence in which the three characters have acted. The Serpent is cut down—he now has to crawl on his belly to move. In addition, mutual loathing is installed between all snakes and all people in the future, poisoning any prospect of their renewed contact (Genesis 3:14–15). Human females are to endure increased pain in giving birth as well as submission to the husbands (Genesis 3:16), while men will toil to feed themselves.

The next phase of the narrative, however, shows how much Yahweh's response has failed to address the situation. The fruit has been eaten. Knowledge has been absorbed by Adam and Eve. And for all Yahweh's retribution, no one has yet died. That is, Yahweh fails to deal with the problem of disseminated self-knowledge, just as he does not follow through on his threat to Adam. Instead, he actually clothes Adam and Eve with garments of hide (Genesis 3:21), more permanent than their initial covering of leaves. He compensates for their self-consciousness; improvisation makes up for a lack of planning.

Yahweh's actions and his inactions eloquently express his character. He does not kill Adam and Eve for eating the forbidden fruit. The same generosity that caused Yahweh to make a tree of Knowledge prevented him from following through on his threat to kill the creatures he had made when they ate from it. Yahweh's character is generous, literally to a fault.

But Yahweh also shows a temper. The Serpent's condemnation to eating dust, the woman's agony in giving birth, man's thankless work in the fields have nothing directly to do with the issue of self-knowledge. Yahweh's reactions are more punitive than productive. Meanwhile, the Yahwists' audience still has not been told why Yahweh is so sensitive to the acquisition of self-knowledge.

Once his initial, stormy retribution has been announced, Yahweh's next action exactly conveys the source of his distress:

> Yahweh God said, "Look, Adam has become like one of us, knowing good and evil. And now, so he does not also put forth hand and take from the tree of life and live forever...." Yahweh God sent him from the Garden of Eden to work the earth from which he had been taken. (Genesis 3:22–23)

The focus of concern now is the status of humanity, and nothing else. The Serpent and his cunning are forgotten.

The narrative does not even say what became of the special intelligence of this smartest of creatures, or what became of his power of speech. Nor does it attend to the differentiation of women and men, which Yahweh has just amplified. All is reduced to Adam, in his role as the archetype of humanity. Yahweh, as the archetype of divinity, and speaking on behalf of all divinities, declares that there is to be a separating barrier between himself and his creatures that cannot be breached, no matter what the degree of his own generosity.

The Yahwists set out the impenetrability of this barrier with vivid imagery:

> He drove Adam out, and settled the Cherubim
> east of the Garden of Eden, and the flame of the
> sword—brandished to guard the way to the tree of
> Life. (Genesis 3:24)

People might absorb knowledge and possess self-consciousness, but they would always know that, unlike God, they were not and could not ever be eternal. Eternity was a privilege that Yahweh guards jealously for himself. Yahweh's Cherubim prevent access to what is to be his, not humanity's.

The close of the account of Yahweh's reaction to Eve and Adam eating from the Knowledge-tree is so fearsome, the audience might expect it is also to be somehow final. Since the expulsion from the Garden is definitive, people's removal from Yahweh's presence might seem to follow. Yet that is not the case. Yahweh is back in easy, direct contact with the children of Adam and Eve, even east of Eden.

Abel and Cain enjoy an access to Yahweh that is comparable to Adam and Eve's. Indeed, the brothers enjoy the additional benefit of being able to offer sacrifice. Yahweh's preference for the delectable offering of sheep becomes the source of deadly strife between the brothers, and in this sense Yahweh misjudges Cain at least as badly as he has misjudged Adam and Eve: while generous to people beyond measure, and angry with them when they let him down, Yahweh never appears to have taken the full measure of his own creation when it comes to human beings, carrying painful implications for them and constant demands on him.

Cain, indeed, comes into focus as the most fully formed human character in the narrative precisely in his resistance to Yahweh, his complaint that being cursed for killing his brother will result in his own death as a nomad at the hands of other men (Genesis 4:13–14). Yahweh protects him with his mark, so the way is set for Cain's foundation of cities and the emergence of civilization (Genesis 4:15–24). But a new separation from Yahweh, a psychological barrier more tangible than the Cherubim and the flaming sword far away, east of Eden, has now also been erected. Yahweh still has taken no life, but Cain has. That act means, as Cain openly says, that he has hidden himself and has been hidden from the face of Yahweh (Genesis 4:14). Never again will there be the direct, physical, person-to-person exchange between people and Yahweh that had characterized life in Eden.

Yahweh still existed, the archetype of divinity corresponding to Adam as the archetype of humanity. But when Cain departed from Yahweh's presence to dwell in

Nod, farther east again from Eden (Genesis 4:16), this new migration marked humanity's exile not only from Eden but also from proximity to and intimacy with God. Now people might call on Yahweh's name (Genesis 4:26) as they continued to offer sacrifice, but they had also entered a new, lonelier mode of living, with the awareness that blood was on their hands and God no longer walked among them in the cool of the evening.

NOTE:

For a short survey of how God is designated, see Dana M. Pike, "The Name and Titles of God in the Old Testament," *Religious Educator* 11.1 (2010) 17-31. A historical and archaeological study is available in Mark S. Smith, *The Early History of God: Yahweh and Other Deities in Ancient Israel:* The Biblical Resource Series (Grand Rapids: Ecrdmans, 2002).

7.

Eden
The Unbroken Presence

A river flows out of Eden to water the Garden, and there divides and becomes four headwaters. GENESIS 2:10

EDEN AS A place is not only the background of the account of the first family; for the Yahwists it is also the generative point of human life itself:

> Yahweh God planted a Garden in Eden, toward the east, and put the Adam that he had formed there. And from the ground Yahweh God made grow every tree that is pleasant to sight and good for food, and the Tree of Life in the middle of the Garden, and the Tree of the Knowledge of good and evil. (Genesis 2:8–9)

At this very first mention, this Garden is said to be "in Eden." It is a place of nourishment and delight, so it comes as no surprise that the Hebrew word *'Eden* actually means "pleasure," "luxury," or "delight."

The Greek translation of the Bible, the Septuagint, refers to the Garden as a *paradeisos*, which is why the term "Paradise" can also refer to this surreally flourishing place. Later Rabbinic literature also picked the term up (as *pardes*). "Eden," "Garden," and "Paradise" are all terms that speak of the primal blessing of all humanity, and indeed the entire creative order, but they also mark that blessing as beyond human reach.

Still, that is not because, in the mind of the ancient culture that produced the story, Eden is simply metaphorical or that it exists in a purely spiritual dimension. In reference to an actual place, the Yahwists also speak of the geographical location of the Garden, "in Eden to the east" (Genesis 2:8). That makes Paradise an eastern region within Eden, but does not quite openly say where Eden itself is. The reference "to the east" might suggest where Eden itself is as well as where the Garden lay within Eden, so that implies that the Yahwists speak in relation to their own position, within the Kingdom of David and Solomon, and probably in Jerusalem.

In their imagination, a giant river flows from Eden in order to water the Garden. From that point, the river divides in four, so as to become the headwaters of the four great rivers of the world:

> A river flows out of Eden to water the Garden, and
> there divides and becomes four headwaters. The
> name of the first is Pishon, which goes about all
> the land of Havilah, where there is gold—and the
> gold of that land is good, and bdellium and onyx.
> The name of the second is Gihon; it goes about
> all the land of Cush. The name of the third river
> is Rapid; it goes east of Assyria. The fourth river is
> Euphrates. (Genesis 2:10-14)

The rivers' names—Pishon, Gihon, Rapid (*hideqel*, known as the Tigris in Greek), and Euphrates—point to where they are. The last two are familiar to usage today, but the Pishon and and Gihon need to be identified. The Pishon is described as flowing through the land of Havilah, where there is fine gold, bdellium, and onyx (Genesis 2:11-12). The last precious items mentioned are associated with the Arabian Peninsula in the experience of the Yahwists, and that would make the river a reference to the Wādī al-Ḥamḍ or perhaps the Wādī al-Rummah. Indeed, because the Pishon is described as going about the whole land, the designation seems to be an interrelated series of streams. The second river, the Gihon, goes about the whole land of

Cush (Genesis 2:13), that is Africa, which means that river is the Nile.

The challenge today, of course, is to imagine a single source for the headwaters of the river systems of Egypt and Sudan (the Nile or Gihon), Saudi Arabia (the great Wādīs or Pishon), and Iraq (the Tigris and Euphrates rivers). Quite aside from the issues of changing elevations and the directional flow of water, a common point of supply for all those rivers seems to be a geographical impossibility. This situation is a more extreme version of what we faced in understanding the Serpent in the Yahwists' account. They referred to a mythical Serpent to explain how real snakes came to be and why they are at continual odds with people. In a comparable move, they also explain how all the great rivers of their time came into existence from one source.

What seems like a geographical impossibility might best to understood as the Yahwists thinking mythically. Just as the mythological Serpent no longer exists, so the rivers continue to flow although Eden has become inaccessible. Snakes are a trace of the Serpent, just as the rivers are a trace of Eden. But that understanding does not correspond to the way the Yahwists frame the matter in their own words. They do not speak of the distant past, but of present reality introduced by a participle in the present tense. The description is emphatic, that the great river that feeds all the world's important rivers, the primordial current that feeds the Garden and there divides into four, contin-ues to flow.

The Yahwists describe, not merely the world as it was in their minds in the distant past, but the world as it existed when they lived. To them the great rivers of the world were continuing forces, necessary to life. Even in places dependent on rainfall, awareness of the vital importance of floodplains was well known. That is what had made the great difference in the emergence of empires in Egypt and Mesopotamia. Indeed, this is precisely what the Yahwists reflect, when they describe how God could make Adam in the first place. Before there was any rain, Yahweh made water available so that earth could be shaped into the form of the person who tilled the earth:

> A flood went up from the earth, and watered all
> the face of the ground. (Genesis 2:6)

The Akkadian word "flood" (not to be confused with a later Arabic term for "mist") probably lies behind the Hebrew text, connecting it with Assyria, one of the regions the Yahwists mention in their description of the great rivers. What once happened in Eden, at the very outset of creation, was replicated every year by the great riv-ers of the world, and that replication made agriculture possible, even in times of drought. Floodplains were so vital that the Yahwists imagine them existing before there was any rain.

What was idyllic in Eden continued in the flooding of rivers. It ensured that grain could be grown in Egypt, fruit in Assyria and Babylonia, and resinous plants such as bdellium in Arabia. In their minds, Yahweh also produced rain, but rivers represented an incalculable blessing—they seemed to flow independently of rainfall, which makes the location of Eden all the more baffling.

This geographical riddle has resulted in surprising suggestions, especially after the discovery of "the New World," which held out the hope that Eden might be discovered, that Paradise might still exist on earth. The great explorers knew their Bible, as did their patrons, and once Europeans understood that the world was a globe, all the references to moving east in Genesis could be taken to imply that originally Eden lay much farther to the west—indeed, from a European point of view, across the ocean. Sir Walter Raleigh resisted such arguments, and kept the focus on the Near East; he could not, of course, resolve how Eden's river could be the source of the great rivers so clearly set forth in Genesis. Speculation, however, was only natural after the shape of the world had changed, and it continued well into the nineteenth century, when, for example, Eden was associated with Missouri by Joseph Smith.

One of the most prominent efforts to locate Eden—to

find Paradise—was that of Christopher Columbus. His thinking is representative of his period in one respect, but his speculations about the location of Eden are worth looking at because they were aligned to where Eden was located in the mind of the Yahwists.

In 1498, when Columbus was making his third voyage, he encountered freshwater off the coast of what we now call Venezuela. Ignorant of South America, he concluded that a huge torrent must be rolling in from Paradise. As he remarked: "If the water of which I speak does not proceed from there, from the earthly Paradise, the wonder is even greater, because I do not believe that a river as big and deep is known anywhere else in the world."

Not realizing that he was dealing with an entirely new continent and its rivers (in this case, the Orinoco) was, of course, one reason for the conclusion that Columbus reached. Another was that, sailing west of the Azores, his observations convinced him that the shape of the earth revealed itself as different from what he had expected: "Each time I sailed from Spain to the Indies, I found that when I reached a point a hundred leagues west of the Azores, the heavens, the stars, and the temperature of the air and the waters of the sea abruptly changed." Such changes, he concluded, must be the result of a change of elevation, and he concluded that "the seas sloped upward." Those deductions, in turn, caused him to doubt whether the world was spherical at all: "I have found such great irregularities that I have come to the following conclusions concerning the world: that it is not round as they describe it, but the shape of a pear, which is round everywhere except the stalk, where it juts out a long way ... like a woman's nipple."

Laurence Bergreen describes these findings as an "upwelling from his unconscious ruminations," and there is no doubt that Columbus's mental state was febrile during much of the third voyage as a consequence of ill health and anxiety. But his unconscious mind was not the only source of his thinking.

As Genesis describes Eden, it is the source of a river that feeds the Garden on its east, from which point it divides and serves as the headwaters of the global series of rivers. By Columbus's time, of course, the number of known rivers had multiplied and massive space to the west had been opened up in geographical imagination, not least as a result of his own voyages. The Yahwists evidently did not design their description to take account of discoveries of a later millennium, and Columbus made the simple mistake that many generations of interpreters have, in expecting a logical finding to emerge from inserting contemporaneous information into an ancient pattern of thought. But within that mistaken application, Columbus also acted upon a feature of the text of Genesis that is often overlooked.

As described by the Yahwists, the Garden is the source of the world's rivers. Since they are located between Egypt and Mesopotamia on the west and east, and Assyria and Saudi Arabia on the north and south, it is natural to think of this ur-source of all river waters as lying in that territory. But it simply is not there. A way around the problem, noted by Sir Walter Raleigh, is to surmise that the flood in the time of Noah changed the topography of the earth so much that Eden and the Garden have been lost. Even lost, however, the text makes them the origin of the great rivers, which is precisely why Columbus thought he found Paradise. He was prepared for that thought, because he had also concluded that he had been sailing in such a way that he was rising in elevation. The headwaters of the world's rivers, in other words, are not at the same level as the sources of each of them, but derive from a massive infusion of waters from above.

Although Columbus had succumbed to a geographical anachronism, he also saw that the Yahwists were not working with only two dimensions in their cosmology: they conceived of height as well as width and length. For them, Eden and the Garden covered an enormous space, and their waters roared in to make up the headwaters of every major known river. That meant that only an upward movement could bring people anywhere near to Paradise and Eden, just the change Columbus had noted in his log of the

131

voyage near the Azores. As an observation of his position, he was in error; as a reader of the text of Genesis, Columbus was correct.

The Yahwists knew very well that water runs downhill and that the mammoth amount of water that runs through the world's rivers could not be hidden on the earth between Mesopotamia and Israel; in their imagination, then, Eden was simply higher than the level they lived on. While the ground was cursed in their experience from the time of Adam's disobedience, once it had yielded food and enjoyment effortlessly. That was the literally higher ground that Yahweh himself inhabited, from which humanity had been expelled.

Columbus's insight about the text was not original. The thought that Eden was a level above the earth on which people presently live was frequently explored in Antiquity. The approach had the advantage of making Eden a continuing reality, without reducing it to a confined space. When Adam was driven out of Eden, Yahweh "settled the Cherubim east of the Garden of Eden, and the flame of the sword—brandished to guard the way to the tree of Life (Genesis 3:24)." The "settling" of the Cherubim is described with a verb that denotes a directional action downward, designed to prohibit access to Eden above.

Elsewhere in the Yahwists' epic, the assumption prevails that Yahweh's natural abode is above humanity. Yahweh is described as coming down to see the Tower of

Babel (Genesis 11:5) and confusing language. The story takes up some of the same themes as the exclusion from Eden, on the assumption that Yahweh does not want people to be on his same level literally, any more than he does intellectually. He is to remain above; they, below.

The division between the above and the below is also natural where it concerns the provision of water. At the time of Noah's flood, God releases inordinate rain from the heavens (Genesis 7:4, 11). Whether in the form of rain or the world's great rivers, Yahweh is the ultimate source of water. People are excluded from the Garden, but water still flows from its paradisal source.

The world of Columbus was smaller than ours, and the world of the Yahwists was smaller still—from Egypt to Babylon and from Arabia to Assyria, roughly equivalent to the Near East. Within that world, the Yahwists located the entry point to the Garden of Eden above them. It was, quite simply, the place where the Cherubim was stationed, guarding access with a sword of flame. Those who depict Paradise in purely mythic terms see that as fantasy, but for the Yahwists Cherubim were a daily reality.

The Ark of the Covenant, already mentioned in our discussion, depicted Cherubim as his sentinels:

The Cherubim shall be spreading their wings upward, overshadowing the Ark-cover with their

133

wings, their faces toward each another; the faces
of the Cherubim shall be toward the Ark-cover.
(Exodus 25:20)

The same beasts that guard the entry into Eden guard
the Ark of the Covenant in its resting place in the Holy of
Holies in the Temple in Jerusalem. Not only was the Ark
decorated by Cherubim, there were statues of Cherubim in
the sanctuary itself, guardians of God's abode. The presence of the Ark made Jerusalem unique among cities: a
center of power and commerce that was also the center of
sanctity, the place where God dwelt. The Cherubim domi-
nated the small space of the Holy of Holies, each of them
ten cubits high, upward of fifteen feet, with each wing the
same length. The description of how Solomon arranged the
Sanctuary makes this plain:

> In the Sanctuary he made two Cherubim of olive
> tree, ten cubits high, five cubits a wing for the
> first Cherub, and five cubits a wing for the sec-
> ond Cherub: ten cubits from wings' end to wings'
> end.... The height of one Cherub was ten cubits,
> and so the second. He put the Cherubim inside
> the inner house, and they extended the wings of
> the Cherubim, so the wing of one Cherub touched
> a wall, and the wing of the second Cherub was

touching the second wall. Their wings in the middle of the house were touching, wing to wing. He overlaid the Cherubim with gold. (1 Kings 6:23–28)

They overshadowed this holiest of places, where the Ark was lodged, a hall decorated with engravings of more Cherubim, palm trees, and flowers; even the floor was decked with gold.

The mention of the Cherubim marks a key connection between the structure of the Temple and the Garden in Eden. That is also the case in the figures of palm trees and flowers, as if features of the Garden are taken up as motifs of the Temple. If deliberate, that would mean that the Temple functions as a stylized Eden, its counterpart on the level of ordinary human beings. Precisely that has been suggested, and the evidence as a whole supports the suggestion.

God walks about in Eden (Genesis 3:8) and in his Sanctuary (Leviticus 26:12; Deuteronomy 23:14; 2 Samuel 7:6–7). No other places are described in these terms, which made the Sanctuary unique on earth.

In addition to being guarded by Cherubim in the manner of the Garden, the Temple was also directionally oriented, in relation to the rising of the sun (Ezekiel 8:16), so that its principal entrance was toward the east, as was the Garden's (Genesis 3:24). In the Israelite orientation, "east" means "in front"; it was the vector that grounded all the possible directions.

The menorah of the Temple is carefully described in Exodus 25:31–40, and leaves no doubt but that the references to branches and flowers and petals and blossoms and leaves carry forward the motifs of Eden to the point that the menorah appears a counterpart to the Life-tree.

Just as Adam is created to "till and keep" the garden (Genesis 2:15), those same verbs are used of the sacrificial work of the Sanctuary on the part of the Levites (Numbers 3:7–8; 8:26; 18:5–6).

The correspondence between Eden and Jerusalem extended to the rivers mentioned in the opening chapters of Genesis. Although Jerusalem was landlocked, Israelites celebrated the existence of a "river whose streams make glad the city of God, the holy habitation of the Most High" (Psalm 46:4). One of Jerusalem's streams is called the Gihon (1 Kings 1:33, 38, 45), which appears as the Nile in biblical Cush within Genesis (2:13), so that Eden's tributary corresponds to Jerusalem's water source.

Gold features prominently in the description of Solomon's Temple and is singled out in another of Eden's tributaries, the Pishon (Genesis 2:11). Bdellium is also mentioned, which is compared to *manna* (in Numbers 11:7), and onyx features prominently in priestly attire

(Exodus 25:7; 28:9-14, 20; cf. 1 Chronicles 29:2) in the Temple.

Since affinities with the Temple have been identified with the rivers Gihon and Pishon, the association of Cherubim with Assyrian culture should be mentioned, in that the Tigris is mentioned with regard to Assyria (Genesis 2:14).

Eden itself functions as an archetype, just as most of the characters in the Garden do, but is described in a way that also insists on its continuing reality. The delightful reality of Eden still impressed itself, in the pure, reliable water of rivers and in the Temple of Solomon, Eden's analogy in Israel's experience.

An archetype, of course, is always purer, stronger, and more beautiful than its copies. For all its beauty, the Sanctuary was not alive in the way that Eden was, and the Garden required no death, as did the work of sacrifice in the Temple. Only when Yahweh decides to clothe Adam and Eve with animal hide does death appear within the narrative in Genesis, and it becomes routinely mentioned only in connection with Abel's offerings. The Garden is where Yahweh and people meet, converse, enjoy, and pursue their work, the ideal counterpart of a Temple, which, however lavish, cannot compete with the reality that it reflects.

When, long after the time of the Yahwists, the Temple was destroyed, the prophet Ezekiel compared the result to the expulsion from Eden (Ezekiel 28:12-19), but then also set out his own vision for how the Temple was to be built again and managed (Ezekiel 40-48), when in its perfection a river would course through it (Ezekiel 47:1-5), as it still courses through Eden. Indeed, such was the durability of the connection between Eden and the Temple that the destruction of the physical edifice only encouraged the hope that the Garden itself would become accessible again to compensate for the loss.

Centuries after Ezekiel, the Temple he had envisioned was destroyed by the Romans. But another seer, John of the Apocalypse, recorded his vision of a new Jerusalem being lowered to the earth; he continues the prophetic recourse to the imagery of Eden (Isaiah 51:3; Ezekiel 28:13; 36:35; Joel 2:3). John's description blends language used for the Garden, the Temple, and Jerusalem in their biblical presentation:

> Then the angel showed me the river of the water of life, bright as crystal, flowing from the throne of God and of the Lamb through the middle of the street of the city. On either side of the river is the tree of life with its twelve kinds of fruit, producing its fruit each month, and the leaves of the tree are for the healing of the nations. (Revelation 22:1-2)

Although the artistry of this seer, John of Patmos, is all his own, and quite unlike that of Ezekiel or of the Yahwists, it would not have been possible apart from the precedent of the Yahwists. They instilled in him, as they had in Ezekiel and in countless others before and after Ezekiel's time, the confidence that a Garden that could not be seen or entered was nonetheless a governing reality more powerful than changes of political and military fortune on the ground. No longer visible or accessible, for the Yahwists and for those of us then and now who have admitted the possibility of what Eden represents, the Garden is palpable, a kind of inner compass, guiding us toward what could be. John of Patmos could imagine that Eden, like God, existed above us. It was an invisible source, both a sanctuary and an enduring promise, inaccessible and unseen but still manifesting continuously in the enduring miracle of life itself and flowing "bright as crystal" in the rivers of the world.

NOTE:

The citations from Columbus's findings derive from Laurence Bergreen, *Christopher Columbus: The Four Voyages, 1491*-1504 (New York: Penguin, 2012), 244. For Walter Raleigh, see his *History of the World in Five Books* (London: Gellingsflower, 1698) 13–22. Joseph Smith's views on Eden's location are discussed in Robert J. Matthews, "Adam-ondi-Ahman," *BYU Studies* 13.1 (1972), 27–35. Connections between the Tree of Life and the Menorah are explored in Carol L. Meyers, *The Tabernacle Menorah: A Synthetic Study of a Symbol from the Biblical Cult*: American Schools of Oriental Research–Dissertation Series, 2 (Missoula:

Scholars Press, 1976), and the Assyrian links of the Cherubim in Raanan Eichler, *The Ark and the Cherubim*: Forschungen zum Alten Testament 146 (Tübingen: Mohr Siebeck, 2021).

EPILOGUE

THE INTENT OF the Yahwists in the opening chapters of Genesis was to show how people came to be as they are in the world. They achieved their aim by telling the stories of Adam and Eve and Cain and Abel, of their interactions with one another and with Yahweh and the Serpent. Eden is a story of human origins. It is for us a strange story, not only prescientific but also pre-monotheistic. The Serpent speaks and Yahweh blunders. People act unpredictably and often come to grief.

The Yahwists' work clashes with the Priestly account of Genesis chapter one, and the dissonance between these two approaches has been obvious to interpreters. Attempts to relate them to one another have produced profoundly influential interpretations through the ages.

Philo of Alexandria, writing at the dawn of the Common Era from his perspective as both a Jew and Platonist, conceived of Genesis 1 as an account of how God created in the pure world of ideas, and of what follows in chapter 2 as the material manifestation of those ideas.

In this way, Philo presented Plato and Moses (whom he supposed was responsible for the Book of Genesis) as mutually interpreting authorities. Plato showed that the reality people inhabit consists not only of the world of perceptions but, more importantly, of another world: that of permanent intellectual and spiritual truth. Moses shared that vision, and was literally blessed with being able to see the reality of the spiritual realm, which is the special gift of prophecy. Philosophy and prophecy together enable the understanding of humanity in its completeness, sharing both similarity to God and kinship with the earth. Armed with his distinction between the spiritual realm and the material realm, both of which human beings inhabit, Philo could explain the strange duality in people's behavior. They are constitutionally Godlike in their minds, but also participate in the animal world with the material of their bodies.

Another school of interpretation, generally referred to as Gnostic, pressed the duality between spiritual and material much further. They portrayed the God of the Yahwists strictly as a secondary figure, emphatically not identical with the all-powerful Creator of the Priestly presentation. Some Gnostics even took Yahweh's divine title in Hebrew, *Adonay Tsebaoth*, which means "Lord of angelic armies," and turned that into a new name in their Greek language, *Ialdabaoth*. In Greek this has no meaning, but it is a deliberate presentation of Yahweh as sounding like nonsense, because he was an imposter. This divine but fraudulent figure saw the true God creating the universe in the spiritual realm and attempted to make a material copy, but could produce only the fallen, corrupt world of matter with all the suffering and injustice that we see around us. One strand of this approach resulted in an attempt to make Christianity into a religion purged of Judaism, since *Ialdabaoth* was the God (or god, really) of the Hebrews. The impulse remains active and is reflected in the popular conception that while God is cruel in the "Old Testament," he is kind in the New Testament. Generalizations of that kind would never survive an attentive reading of the Revelation to John, the last book in the New Testament. Still, they not only persist but flourish.

In their very different ways, Philo's approach and the Gnostic approach both typify the effort to discover a single, coherent reading of traditions that are manifestly divergent. Philo's strategy is synthetic: he assigns some texts to God's heavenly realm and some to humanity's realm on the earth. The Gnostic approach, which flourished between the second and the fourth centuries, is disjunctive, portraying Yahweh as a demigod who attempted to take over the place of the supreme Creator. Each of these strategies has been renewed and adjusted in the history of interpretation, usually in a blended form; Philo and the Gnostics permit us to see how they work in isolation, and in a fairly straight-forward way.

A blended interpretation, which combines the Yahwists' portrayal with the Priestly presentation and also insists on substantial differences, resulted in a surprising conception of Adam in the ancient world. It targets him as a single figure, but one that radically changed between his first appearance as "in the image of God," both male and female (Genesis 1:27), and his reduced stature when he was expelled from the Garden (Genesis 3:21–24). In the Talmud Bavli (Ḥagigah 12a), Rabbi El'azar produced a stunning visual image in teaching that "The first man extended from earth to the firmament," but then was reduced to his present size after the consumption of the fruit. That picture of humanity's tragic loss of literally cosmic stature, from the fifth century, later emerged in Islam, when a *hadith* of the Prophet (collected by Sahih al Bulkhari in the ninth century) states: "Allah created Adam, making him 60 cubits tall." Augustine, the Christian bishop of Hippo of North Africa, took a different approach, which makes Adam's reduction psychological rather than physical. Augustine portrayed Adam as being able not to sin when he was created, but once he did sin by his own choice, he was constituted to keep sinning (*City of God* XXII.30). That is the foundation of Augustine's argument, formulated at the same time that the Talmud made its influence felt in Judaism, for the Christian doctrine of Original Sin.

For all the sense of tragedy that pervades the Yahwists' vision, the Priestly idea of humans being in the image of God also continued to exert a powerful influence. In 1649, John Milton articulated a principle of political freedom derived from the first chapter of Genesis, when he insisted it was obvious that "all men naturally were born free being in the image and resemblance of God himself, and were by privilege above all the creatures, born to command and not to obey." Milton made his argument in writing a tract on behalf of Oliver Cromwell, called *The Tenure of Kings and Magistrates*, to justify the beheading of King Charles I. The mythic force of much of the material in Genesis can be and has been focused in particular cases to produce powerful, sometimes violent policies and actions. In this case, Milton pioneered a claim of fundamental rights that belong to people because they are people, which has proved both disruptive and liberating ever since.

While the continuing presence of the divine image in "all men" emerged after Milton as a principle of the Enlightenment that is echoed in the Declaration of Independence, women tended to be characterized more in terms of the Yahwists' narrative rather than the Priestly conception. What is without question the most influential text in this regard comes from the New Testament:

Indeed Adam was formed first, then Eve. And Adam was not deceived, but the woman was deluded and came into transgression. Yet she will be saved by childbearing, if they remain in faith and love and holiness with sobriety. (1 Timothy 2:13-15)

In this summary of events in Genesis 3, Adam is made into a mere passenger within Eve's deception, and the Serpent is sidelined. Moreover, it is simply assumed that "the woman" stands for all women who are to follow for all time, the "they" who are instructed to bear the consequences of an action in which they did not take part.

Although this clear statement is made in a letter attributed to Paul that was composed only after his death, an earlier letter—which Paul indisputably did write—reflects a different understanding of the significance of Eve in Genesis:

Indeed male is not from woman, but woman from male, since also male was not created for the woman, but woman for the male.... Except: in the Lord's perspective woman is not apart from male nor is male apart from woman, since just as the woman is from the male, so male comes to be

through the woman, and everything is from God.
(1 Corinthians 11:8–9, 11–12)

The difference in these two interpretations comes in part from the degree to which, in 1 Corinthians, the Yahwists' presentation is modified by a principle of equality that derives from the Priestly presentation. In addition, both interpretations selectively ignore prominent features of the narrative: Adam's passive alacrity in consuming the fruit in 1 Timothy, and the whole issue of the Tree of Knowledge in 1 Corinthians.

Interpretations of Genesis are necessarily selective unless the entire text is reproduced in the form of a commentary, and by that point the insight the interpreter seeks to express will be lost in everything else that needs to be said. The examples provided here from Judaic, Muslim, and Christian tradition might easily be multiplied, and their power relies on their being pithy rather than complete. Sometimes an interpreter will simply invoke a name from the text to invoke an eternal principle.

In the second century, the bishop of Sardis in present-day Turkey, named Melito, explained the meaning of Passover in terms of the suffering of Christ. He did that by relating the name of the feast in Greek (*Paskha*) to the Greek verb that means "to suffer" (*paskhein*). But then

Melito presented Christ as the foundation and apex of a deep pattern, beginning with Abel:

> It is he who was in Abel murdered,
> And in Isaac bound,
> And in Jacob exiled,
> And in Joseph sold,
> And in Moses exposed,
> And in the lamb slain,
> And in David persecuted,
> And in the prophets dishonored.

To Melito, Abel was the first paradigm, fulfilled in Christ but also in many others, of the tragic interruption of youthful innocence and promise by corrupt antagonists.

At a later stage, the Quran presents an even nobler portrait of Abel and turns Cain into his dark double. Abel says to his brother (Ma'ida 5:28–29):

> "If you stretch out your hand against me
> To kill me,
> I will not stretch out my hand against you
> To kill you.
> I in fact fear God,
> Lord of all the worlds.
> Indeed, I intend by withholding my hand

That you bear my sin and your own sin,
So that you will become
One of the companions of the fire of hell!
For that is the recompense of the wrongdoers who
are godless in heart."

Like the earliest version of the Yahwists' narrative, the
Quran originated as an oral text, recited by the Prophet
on the basis of angelic disclosure. In its presentation, the
Quran succeeds more than any of the world's Scriptures
in retaining a link with its oral, memorized transmission
prior to writing. Departures from Genesis are understood
to restore the intended meaning and the authentic form of
revelation.

Expansions of this kind are at one level obvious
deviations from the original text, and yet precisely in their
deviation they express a fresh insight into the Yahwists'
characterization. Over time, the mythic dimensions of the
events concerning Eden were in fact expanded by interpreters. Some of these innovations have entered into the
world of what is considered traditional, so as to create the
expectation that the original text of Genesis must agree
with what is actually a comparatively recent belief.

Despite efforts designed to meet traditionalist expec-
tations, however, the pages of Genesis never, for example, depict Satan in the way that John Milton sees him in

Paradise Lost. In his portrayal, only after expulsion from heaven did he approach Eve in the form the text of Genesis identifies (Book I, 34–40).

> Th' infernal Serpent; he it was, whose guile
> Stird up with Envy and Revenge, deceiv'd
> The Mother of Mankinde, what time his Pride
> Had cast him out from Heav'n, with all his Host
> Of Rebel Angels, by whose aid aspiring
> To set himself in Glory above his Peers,
> He trusted to have equal'd the most High.

This represents a mixture of Genesis with its interpretation in 1 Timothy, and even more with the portrayal in the Revelation of John, the last book of the New Testament, of Satan's war with God. In setting that combat in the primordial time before human history began, Milton also shows the influence of how Augustine portrayed the fall of Satan in *The City of God* 12.1–9. Puritan interpretation, of which Milton was a master (serving, before he composed *Paradise Lost*, as "Secretary for Foreign Tongues" under Oliver Cromwell, who brought Puritan influence to its zenith in England), delighted in the layering and aggregation of biblical passages into vivid new portrayals of the meanings involved. That creativity does not in any way make Milton a bad interpreter but neither does it imply that the Yahwists' approach was in some way defective by not anticipating later interpretations. Rather, the Yahwists and John Milton, with many intermediaries in between, take up a millennial dialogue concerning the nature of the forces that ultimately blocked humanity from the "blissful Seat" (as Milton calls Eden in I, 5) that God had provided for them.

The power of the Yahwists has deeply influenced their interpreters, both within the Bible and after the Bible, and interpretation has been engaged from many different kinds of perspective, dogmatic and not. When Laszlo Bito, a fiercely independent intellectual, took up his pen to write *Eden Revisited*, part of his inspiration was to portray Yahweh as a person, not a god, and Cain as hero more than villain. As I remarked to him while he was at work, those decisions represent the continued vibrancy of a Gnostic approach. Not only did Gnostics demote *Ialdebaoth*, they also reversed a standard portrayal of Cain because, after all, his actions brought about the emergence of civilization. Yet the interpersonal intensity of Bito's treatment, with its systematic insistence on explaining all the actions depicted by the Yahwists in human terms, distinguishes his perspective from that of the ancient Gnostics.

Every memorable, notable, or incisive interpretation does not merely repeat the text that is interpreted; the qualities of a reading surface in the subtle interaction between the text and the interpreter's perspective. When a text has been interpreted for several generations, however, there is a tendency for whatever interpretation has emerged as dominant to be identified with the text itself. Whether the initial text is written or oral, and whatever media the interpreters work in, it is easily submerged within the perspective of the interpreting community that preserves it.

Biblical texts, for several reasons, have especially suffered from the tendency of interpretation to appropriate the identity of what is interpreted. The very fact of their age means that, in the case of the oldest examples such as the Yahwists, they have been interpreted for three millennia. Perhaps more important, the fact of being incorporated within the Bible means the texts appear in contexts that were not involved in their production. The special question of the relationship between the Yahwists' work and Priestly presentation has occupied our attention repeatedly, because otherwise the distinctive perspectives of each cannot be disentangled. After the Bible emerged as a collection of texts, its interpretation occurred within new contexts, some at strong variance with one another, including Judaism, Christianity, Islam, and the many microclimates of exegesis within each of them. Recent centuries have seen schools of interpretation that champion particular approaches to reading the texts emerge, including historical criticism, fundamentalism, structuralism, deconstruction, gender studies, and postcolonial theory.

These contexts of interpretation all have their contributions to make, although none of them can claim to be uniquely valid, except by a dogmatic assertion that does not come from the text itself. The value of any reading is determined by how adequately it accounts for the originating text, rather than the alleged superiority of the method of approach. Making an assessment on the basis of the text itself helps to prevent particular interpretations from overwhelming the texts whose meaning they claim to convey. In the case of the Yahwists' narrative, it seems to me that the creative readings that came after are better appreciated when the contribution of the originators has been understood.

Biblical scholarship along the lines of identifying what the Yahwists brought in to the Book of Genesis has in the past tended to be concerned with which specific verses (or parts of verses) they contributed. This necessary work, based on an analysis of language and style that we have reflected on from time to time during this book, can become mechanical when it excludes considering how the Yahwists conveyed a vision of Eden as the matrix of humanity. That Yahwists' vision, and how the Yahwists developed it by means of the characterization of the players in the story, has been the particular concern of this book. That focus permits us to see the Yahwists' perspective, to gather a sense of the setting in which they operated, and to hear their voice as a distinctive part of the millennial dialogue in regard to human origins that they initiated.

Concentration on the very first form of a text can be a trap when it encourages the supposition that only the original version of any text is its authentic form. The Book of Genesis cannot be reduced to its most primitive elements alone, and that has not been the program of this book. Seeing how the Yahwists conceived of human origins in no way negates the Priestly perspective. In fact, both are better appreciated when their individuality is permitted to stand out. The Bible is not written from a single, standard point of view, but represents generations of collecting different kinds of writing, each from its own time and place. Interpretation begins with a readiness to hear each distinctive voice.

The Yahwists invite us to join them in seeing the human condition and its relation to their understanding of the divine from the point of view of the Davidic kingdom during the tenth century BCE. That world repeatedly surfaces in their story. Their reference to the social realities of the time joins with their style of narration and their thoroughly anthropomorphic conception of Yahweh. Their presentation is both persistently alien and deeply familiar.

The pleasure and pain of encountering the First Family derives from their kinship to us. They speak in terms that correspond to the way that we conceive of the world, and they embody continuing realities. They arrive perennially fresh from Eden, where we walked with God and existed in a state of innocence without self-consciousness or shame. We still carry with us our awakening into the burdens and suffering of life, the sense of our separation from the divine and rude departure from an existence of effortlessness and ease. Has the knowledge we've gained been worth it? What would our world look like if we hadn't eaten the fruit?

We still wonder what could have been, and we still yearn for the Eden of the Yahwists. The way back is guarded by the Cherubim and a mobile, flaming sword. We have felt the fire of that sword in our utopian experiments through the ages. And yet we persist. All we need for inspiration is to reenter the text, to read, to be moved, perhaps in spite of ourselves, by its immortal words. The denizens of Eden, and Eden itself, have entered into our collective consciousness, so that the decision we make about how we see them and the choices they made shape both who we are and who we might become.

NOTE:

The close of this book, and indeed the book itself, is designed to pursue an approach to the Bible that accounts for historical and exegetical detail but clearly targets the meanings the contributors intended. Most of the works already cited represent stages in developing that approach. Examples of broader applications includ, David M. Carr, *Holy Resilience: The Bible's Traumatic Origins* (New Haven: Yale University Press, 2014) and John Barton, *A History of the Bible* (New York: Viking, 2019).

NICHOLAS ALTON LEWIS

ABOUT BRUCE CHILTON

Bruce Chilton is one of the foremost scholars in the world of early Christianity and Judaism. He wrote the first critical translation of and commentary for the Aramaic version of Isaiah (*The Isaiah Targum*), as well as academic studies that analyze Jesus in his Judaic context (*A Galilean Rabbi and His Bible*; The *Temple of Jesus*; *Pure Kingdom*). His other principal publications include: *Rabbi Jesus: An Intimate Biography*; *Rabbi Paul: An Intellectual Biography*; *Mary Magdalene: A Biography*; *Resurrection Logic: How Jesus'*

First Followers Believed God Raised Him from the Dead; and, most recently, *The Herods: Murder, Politics, and the Art of Succession*. He has taught in Europe at the universities of Cambridge, Sheffield, and Münster, and in the United States at Yale University (as the first Lillian Claus Professor of New Testament) and Bard College. Currently Bernard Iddings Bell Professor of Philosophy and Religion at Bard, he directs the Institute of Advanced Theology.

Natus Books, founded in 2019, is an imprint of the Institute for Publishing Arts, a 501(c)3 corporation dedicated to challenging and expanding conceptions of human possibility. The Institute is the sponsor of Station Hill Press, since 1977 the publisher of poetry, fiction, translations and non-fiction, primarily in the areas of literary philosophy and mind, body and spirit. Both Natus and Station Hill are distributed by Chicago-based Independent Publishers Group. Natus Books is dedicated to collaborating with religious, political, community and cultural organizations.

159